Guide to the Superior Hiking Trail

Linking people with nature by footpath
along Lake Superior's North Shore

Superior Hiking Trail Association
2010

Guide to the Superior Hiking Trail

Printed in the United States of America
by McNaughton & Gunn, Inc.
First Edition, 1993
Second Edition, 1998
Third Edition, 2001
Fourth Edition, 2004
Fifth Edition, 2007

Cover and text design: Sally Rauschenfels
Map illustrations: Matt Kania, Diane Desotelle
Cover photo: Jay Steinke
Title page photo: Sam Cook
Illustrations: Dover

*Although the editors and publisher have researched all sources
to ensure the accuracy and completeness of the information
contained in this book, we assume no responsibility for errors,
inaccuracies, omissions or any inconsistency herein.*

ISBN: 978-0-9636598-6-6

10 9 8 7 6 5 4 3 2 1

The Superior Hiking Trail

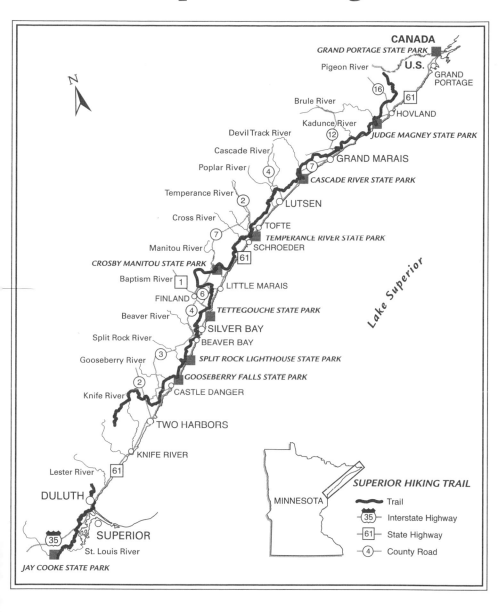

CANADA
GRAND PORTAGE STATE PARK
Pigeon River
U.S.
GRAND PORTAGE
16
61
Brule River
HOVLAND
Kadunce River
JUDGE MAGNEY STATE PARK
Devil Track River
12
Cascade River
GRAND MARAIS
Poplar River
4
7
CASCADE RIVER STATE PARK
Temperance River
2
LUTSEN
Cross River
TOFTE
7
TEMPERANCE RIVER STATE PARK
Manitou River
SCHROEDER
61
CROSBY MANITOU STATE PARK
Baptism River
1
LITTLE MARAIS
FINLAND
6
Beaver River
4
TETTEGOUCHE STATE PARK
SILVER BAY
Split Rock River
BEAVER BAY
Gooseberry River
3
SPLIT ROCK LIGHTHOUSE STATE PARK
GOOSEBERRY FALLS STATE PARK
2
CASTLE DANGER
Knife River
TWO HARBORS
KNIFE RIVER
Lester River
61
DULUTH
35
SUPERIOR
St. Louis River
JAY COOKE STATE PARK

Lake Superior

MINNESOTA

SUPERIOR HIKING TRAIL

Trail
35 — Interstate Highway
61 — State Highway
4 — County Road

Foreword

What I remember best is squatting on a shoulder of rock, gazing out at the Poplar River Valley. The valley was lush and green and rolled on forever. Down the middle of it meandered the river itself, a reflection of horseshoe bends flowing cool and blue through the lowlands.

I was hot and sweaty from a morning on the trail, and I don't know how long I sat there. I couldn't tell you what I thought about, other than that it was one of the finest places I've ever shed a pack and let the breeze glide over my skin.

Doubtless hundreds of hikers have had the same feeling at a hundred different places along the Superior Hiking Trail.

It is that good.

We owe a large debt to the visionaries who conceived this trail and to Tom Peterson, who must have worn out several pairs of boots choosing its route. It is difficult to hike any distance on the trail without emerging in awe of Peterson's genius and dedication.

And now we have Andrew Slade and a whole crew of other volunteers to thank for this mile-by-mile companion piece to the trail itself. It was a book begging to be written, but which was going to require the spirit of a naturalist and the research of a scientist.

The book's production team, with the help of geologists, botanists, ornithologists, historians and camping experts, has given us a compendium of information about the Superior Hiking Trail. The book's format is hiker-friendly. Its detail is complete. And it fits in a backpack.

This book can help you park your car, arrange a shuttle, find water or find a camp. It'll tell you where you're likely to see a moose or to see Isle Royale, where you're treading in the voyageurs' footsteps and why the rock fractures the way it does along the Split Rock River.

The information in this guide will not weigh you down. It will answer a lot of your questions and free you to get on with the walking.

And maybe one day you'll find yourself doing what I was doing that July morning, what backpacking guru Colin Fletcher calls "sitting on a peak and thinking of nothing at all except perhaps that it is a wonderful thing to sit on a peak and think of nothing at all."

Good reading. Happy walking.

— *Sam Cook*

Table of Contents

Superior Hiking Trail Section Descriptions

Day Hike Opportunities Begin Here

Day Hike Opportunities Continue, Backpack Camping Opportunities Begin Here

Description of the Superior Hiking Trail

T HE SUPERIOR HIKING TRAIL (SHT), built and maintained by the Superior Hiking Trail Association (SHTA), is a footpath routed mostly along the ridgeline overlooking Lake Superior on Minnesota's North Shore. The SHT is 277 miles long. The southernmost segment is 42 miles through Jay Cooke State Park and the city of Duluth and provides only day hiking opportunities. From Duluth to Fox Farm Road, west of Two Harbors, there is a gap in the SHT where trail construction is ongoing. The next segment is 235 miles long from the Fox Farm Road trailhead to the Otter Lake Road trailhead just short of the Canadian border. This segment has both day hiking and backpack camping opportunities.

At its lowest point, the trail goes along the lakeshore, which is 602 feet above sea level. At its highest point, in the hills of the Jackson Lake area, the trail is 1,829 feet above sea level and more than 1,200 feet above Lake Superior. It is characterized by ascents to rock outcroppings and cliffs, and descents into numerous river and creek valleys crossed by bridges.

The SHT is designed as a footpath only, comprised mainly of an 18-inch treadway through a clearing approximately four feet wide. The use of motorized vehicles, mountain bikes and horses is prohibited on the trail. The steepness and narrowness of the SHT in most areas make it unsuitable for cross-country skiing, although snowshoe travel is possible in many places.

The SHT traverses a rich variety of terrain and habitat types. The transitions from oak, basswood and maple to the boreal forests of balsam, pine, spruce, cedar and tamarack is interrupted by regrowth forest of aspen and birch. Grassy clearings, products of lumbering operations and forest fires, provide interesting variation from the more prevalent woodland scenes. Panoramic overlooks of Lake Superior, the Sawtooth Mountains and inland forests, lakes and rivers are abundant along the length of the SHT. At many points, the trail follows rivers and creeks, often for distances of a mile or more, showcasing waterfalls and rapids, bends and deep gorges where rushing water over thousands of years has cut into layers of ancient volcanic bedrock.

Each season of the year offers its own rewards for the SHT hiker. Wildflowers are especially prevalent in the spring, but some varieties are evident throughout the hiking season. Fortunate spring hikers will see and hear many species of songbirds. Spring is also the time for the unique color of emerging leaves. Summer brings the long hiking days and the sort of heat that makes a dip in one of the cool rivers all the more inviting. Wild blueberries and raspberries provide a special mid-summer treat at many points along the SHT. Fall is a symphony of colors and smells on the SHT, and drier weather and fewer biting insects make it the friendliest time of year to hike. Winter is a time of quiet magic on the SHT, and snowshoeing the trail is increasingly popular.

Wildlife abounds; encounters with deer are common, as well as sightings of moose, beaver, black bear, eagles and grouse.

The trail crosses national forest and state park lands; state, county and city property; and private property. The SHT reaches nearly to the Canadian border where the Swamp River meets the Pigeon River, and along its route connects and traverses eight state parks. Many property owners—individuals and corporations, in addition to governmental units—have granted easements or permits for the SHT to cross their land. In some areas, special restrictions apply. Hikers must observe all posted restrictions (such as requirements to stay on the trail through private property, and prohibitions on fires, camping or hunting). The privilege to use these private lands depends upon the cooperation of trail users and their respect for special restrictions.

The one constant feature of the SHT, and the characteristic that distinguishes it from other trails, is the presence of Lake Superior—the legendary lake the Ojibwa named Gitchi Gami, or "big water." Although the distance to the big lake varies considerably along the SHT, its presence is always felt. Sometimes "lake effect" weather brings cool breezes and moisture in to shore, though in summer it may be 20 degrees warmer just over the ridge. In wintertime, the lake moderates temperatures near the shore. The SHT features many spectacular views of Lake Superior, as well as many more subtle views through the trees, allowing the hiker an endless selection of spots to rest, lunch and meditate against the backdrop of the lake's many moods and colors. From some vantage points, the Wisconsin/Michigan shoreline is visible on the horizon; other views feature islands—Isle Royale on the northern part of the SHT and the Apostle Islands on the southern end.

Lake Superior itself is the largest freshwater lake in the world by surface area. It is 350 miles long and 160 miles wide at its farthest dimensions. Its average depth is 489 feet, and its maximum depth is 1,333 feet. As a part of the Great Lakes shipping corridor, it is the inland terminus of a commercial shipping trade that reaches to the East Coast and across the Atlantic Ocean. After the ice departs in spring, until sometime in January, the hiker can spot big vessels on the lake—the ore and grain freighters that carry Midwestern exports to points east, and the "salties" that come from ports across the ocean. In the summer months when the lake is more placid, hikers can see sailboats, charter fishing boats and even small motorboats, canoes and kayaks near the shore. Lake Superior's shipwrecks are legendary and are documented at places such as the Split Rock Lighthouse Visitor Center and in books and paintings found in the many galleries and shops along the North Shore. Lake Superior, with its history and its beauty, gives the SHT a unique and unforgettable character.

Accessing and Using the Trail

There are no permits or fees required to hike on the Superior Hiking Trail. In the Jay Cooke State Park and Duluth area, the SHT is accessible from I-35, Highway 23, and city streets. On the North Shore, it is accessible from Highway 61. The state parks along the North Shore provide access to the SHT, as do state, county and forest roads that intersect Highway 61. Some but not all access points are marked by brown highway signs that say "Superior Hiking Trail" and may have the SHT logo on them. The distance between trailheads with parking lots—most from five to ten miles apart—makes the SHT easily divisible into one-way day hikes, accomplished by leaving a vehicle at one trailhead and driving a second vehicle to the next trailhead to begin the hike.

Superior Shuttle. Hiking parties without two vehicles can use the Superior Shuttle service. The Superior Shuttle runs Fridays, Saturdays and Sundays mid-May to mid-October, stopping at most trailheads on the North Shore twice a day on a fixed schedule. Reservations are not needed to use the Superior Shuttle.

It may also be possible to arrange a shuttle through local resorts or outfitters.

Day hikes. Numerous other possibilities exist for day hikes and loop hikes, some employing state park, city or national forest trails. Of course, a hike to a point on the trail with a return along the same trail is never a disappointment. The vista you missed over your shoulder on the way is revealed in all its splendor on the way out. Rewarding day hikes are spotlighted in the chapter entitled "The Best of the Superior Hiking Trail," on page 38.

Hikers planning a hike should allow one hour for every one to two miles. Day-hikers should carry a pack with adequate water (river and lake water along the SHT must be treated before it is consumed), snacks, sunscreen, bug repellent, toilet paper, compass, flashlight, and an extra clothing layer and rain gear if conditions warrant. Remember that weather conditions can change rapidly; dark storm clouds and chilly winds sometimes move in quickly and unexpectedly on what began as a warm, cloudless day. Hikers planning to hike more than one or two hours should be prepared for weather changes.

Trail marking. Trailheads all have signs with mileages to the next trailheads. There are occasional mileage signs along the trail, but they are infrequent.

The entire trail is paint blazed. The main SHT is marked by blue painted rectangles. Spur trails and overlook trails are marked by white painted rectangles. Turns in the trail are marked with two rectangles, with one slightly higher than the other. The higher one indicates the direction the trail turns. SHT logo markers are also posted at

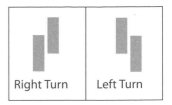

| Right Turn | Left Turn |

places along the trail, mostly at intersections with roads or other trails.

Maps. Hikers should always carry a map when on the trail. There are places where the SHT crosses other trails and roads that may be confusing, and times when the trail is covered with leaves or snow. The SHTA publishes and sells several types of maps of the trail. These can be purchased at the SHTA office/store in Two Harbors, by calling the SHTA office or by ordering them online. State park visitor centers and stores also sell the maps.

Dogs. Dogs must be on a leash at all times—especially in popular areas where other hikers are likely to be encountered. Dog owners should remember that although their dogs may be friendly, there may be people hiking on the trail who are afraid of dogs. Dogs also may frighten wildlife, and vice versa.

Pack animals. Pack animals are not allowed on the SHT.

Trail conditions by season. Trail conditions are posted regularly on the SHTA website so hikers should be sure to use this service as part of trip planning. In general, each season on the SHT has its own rewards, but each has its own cautions for trail users. The SHT is generally not dry enough to hike on until early May. Hikers out before this time need to be prepared for wet feet and blisters. Campfire bans are also sometimes posted on the trail in the spring.

About mid-July some of the small streams that are water sources for some of the campsites dry up and water must be obtained before reaching the campsite. There are sometimes campfire bans in the summer as well.

Fall brings hunting seasons—grouse, bear, moose and deer are hunted in the north woods. Many sections of the SHT are closed during the firearms deer season for two weeks in November. A list of closures is available at the SHTA office and on the website. Signs are posted at trailheads to advise of trail closings. Even on sections of the trail that are not posted closed, hikers should be sure to wear blaze orange clothing and stay alert during hunting seasons.

Winter visitors should keep in mind that snowshoeing takes much longer than hiking. Also, some of the trailhead parking lots are not plowed.

Backpacking. The SHT is ideally suited for long-distance hiking. There are 86 backcountry campsites along the SHT. Each campsite has two to eight tent pads, a fire ring and a backcountry latrine. There are no reservations, fees or permits required to use these campsites. Parties are required to share campsites. Since the trail crosses so much private land and state park land, and often land ownership is not indicated, backpackers must camp only at the designated campsites. Backpackers who camp at state park campgrounds must pay required fees. There are no SHT campsites in the Duluth section of the trail. For additional information about backpacking on the SHT, and tips for overnight trips, see the "Backpacking" chapter.

Lodge-to-lodge hiking. For the long-distance hiker who prefers more amenities, lodge-to-lodge hiking is available through Boundary Country Trekking. The hiker needs only a daypack, since lodge staff will shuttle hikers to trail destinations each day.

Guidebook use. This guidebook is designed to be a functional resource for hikers to plan their adventures on the SHT. In addition to general information about the trail, the guidebook includes a mile-by-mile description of the trail. The text is broken into segments, with a summary description of each trail section, and information on parking, access points and campsites. In addition, the highlights of each segment are featured – rivers, waterfalls, overlooks and other natural features. To enhance the hiking experience, information on natural and human history is also included. Landmarks and points of interest referenced in the text are indicated on the maps in the book as well as the pocket maps that are sold separately.

Useful Information

- Superior Hiking Trail Association (store and office)
  731 7th Ave. (Hwy. 61), PO Box 4, Two Harbors, MN 55616
  218-834-2700; hike@shta.org; www.shta.org

- Lodge to Lodge Hiking Program: Boundary Country Trekking
  1-800-322-8327 or 218-388-4487
  bct@boundarycountry.com
  www.boundarycountry.com

- Superior Shuttle: Information and reservations 218-834-5511
  www.superiorshuttle.com

- Minnesota State Parks Information: 1-888-646-6367
  Reservations: 1-866-857-2757
  www.stayatmnparks.com

- Superior National Forest
  Tofte Ranger Station 218-663-8060
  Gunflint Ranger Station 218-387-1750
  www.fs.fed.us/r9/superior

- Duluth Convention and Visitors Bureau
  1-800-438-5884 or 218-722-4011
  www.visitduluth.com

- RJ Houle Information Center, Two Harbors, MN
  1-800-777-7384 or 218-834-6200
  www.twoharborschamber.com

- Lutsen-Tofte Tourism Association, Tofte, MN
  1-888-616-6784 or 218-663-7804
  www.americasnorthcoast.org

- Grand Marais Visitor Center, Grand Marais, MN
  1-888-922-5000 or 218-387-2524
  www.grandmarais.com

The Superior Hiking Trail Association

THE SUPERIOR HIKING TRAIL ASSOCIATION is a Minnesota non-profit corporation whose members are dedicated to the completion, preservation, and promotion of the Superior Hiking Trail. The original members of the SHTA were the visionaries—federal and state government representatives and local North Shore resort and business owners—who incorporated the SHTA and obtained the first funding to see their vision become a reality. From this small group, membership has grown to approximately 3,300, including members in 37 states, Canada, and four other countries.

Staff and Board of Directors. The SHTA has paid staff working in the office/store in Two Harbors as well as seasonal maintenance contractors. A board of directors consisting of members from a variety of locations, careers, avocations, and age groups meets bimonthly on the North Shore to make policy decisions for the SHTA and oversee the substantive work of the association, including trail maintenance, product sales, hikes and event planning, and publications.

Activities. The most visible activities of the SHTA are the popular organized hikes scheduled throughout the hiking season, including wintertime snowshoe hikes. Hosted by SHTA members and featuring leaders with interpretive skills, such as naturalists, geologists, photographers, and historians, most of the SHTA-sponsored events are one-way day hikes with a group shuttle. The SHTA's hiking program also features backpacking trips of several days. SHTA members also have the opportunity to attend the Annual Meeting, scheduled in May, to participate in a weekend full of hiking, fun, and camaraderie.

Volunteers. Trail maintenance is provided through a system of volunteers. Some have taken responsibility for the upkeep of particular trail sections and campsites. Others participate in scheduled maintenance projects. Scout troops, outdoors clubs, and other organizations have all undertaken trail maintenance responsibilities. Individuals and groups can give something back to the trail by volunteering to help with trail maintenance. There are also opportunities to help with trail construction. SHTA office staff will gladly provide you with information on how you can help.

Office and store. The SHTA office and store is located at 731 7th Ave. (the corner of Highway 61 and 8th Street, in an olive-green Victorian house) in Two Harbors. The store offers a variety of merchandise including guidebooks, maps, t-shirts, sweatshirts, caps, mugs, and other mementos of the SHT. Friendly staff can also answer your questions about the SHT and hike planning. The store is open seven days a week from mid-May to mid-October and Monday through Friday the rest of the year. The mailing address is SHTA, P.O. Box 4, Two Harbors, MN, 55616. The phone number is (218) 834-2700.

Website. A great deal of information is also available at the SHTA website at www.shta.org. The information includes membership information, store items, trip reports, trail condition updates, and links to lodging, gear, and other useful websites.

Membership. The SHTA is a member-based organization of over 3,000 members. The primary monetary support for SHTA activities comes from membership dues and contributions. We invite you to join SHTA to help build and maintain the Superior Hiking Trail. Member benefits include free maps of the trail, *The Ridgeline* newsletter four times a year, and information on guided hikes, maintenance work projects, and the Annual Meeting. The most important benefit is the knowledge you are helping to preserve and protect this wonderful trail. You can join by calling or writing the SHTA office or using the form on the website at www.shta.org.

History of the Trail

THE SUPERIOR HIKING TRAIL was conceived in the mid-1980s as a long-distance footpath, modeled after the Appalachian Trail and other long trails, along the ridgeline overlooking Lake Superior's North Shore from Duluth, Minnesota, to the Canadian border. The Superior Hiking Trail is the realization of an ambitious plan fostered by a group of visionaries—federal, state, and local government employees, artists, resort and business owners, and hiking enthusiasts—who in 1986 incorporated the Superior Hiking Trail Association and made the first request for state funding for trail construction. Three grants from the Legislative Commission on Minnesota Resources (LCMR), each covering a two-year period (1987–89, 1989–91 and 1991–93), were the principal source of funding for early trail construction. In more recent years, planning and construction funding has come from private donations, the St. Louis County Recreation Fund, the Federal Recreation Trail Program, the Duluth-Superior Area Community Foundation, NOAA's Office of Ocean and Coastal Resource Management, in conjunction with Minnesota's Lake Superior Coastal Program, and Minnesota's Local Trail Connection Program. Volunteers have also provided countless hours of trail construction.

The SHT was officially opened with a ceremonial "log-cutting" in July 1987 at Britton Peak on the Sawbill Trail, an event attended by federal, state, and local officials and dignitaries, in addition to the trail's founders. In August 1990, the SHTA sponsored a "Halfway

Celebration" at Gooseberry Falls State Park, commemorating the completion of nearly 140 miles of trail—approximately halfway to the goal of a continuous footpath from Duluth to the Canadian border. This celebration was the culmination of the SHTA's first sponsored backpacking trip, in which a dozen hikers trekked the completed trail in twelve rigorous days. They were greeted by another impressive contingent of dignitaries and well-wishers at Gooseberry Falls State Park.

In September 1991, the SHT was the site of the first "Superior 100" endurance run, in which long-distance "ultra-marathon" runners from around the country competed in a 100-mile race. The race has been run every year since.

The first documented through-hiker of the trail was Paul Hlina in 1995. Paul raised $16,000 in pledges for the SHTA and Wilderness Inquiry as he hiked the length of the trail with crutches due to his paralysis.

Though a relative newcomer to the country's long-distance trails, and a toddler by comparison with its prototype and model, the Appalachian Trail (conceived in 1921 and completed, in its first layout, fifteen years later), the SHT has already won national recognition. It has been featured in countless regional publications and broadcasts and has been the subject of stories in national magazines, such as *Prevention, Walking* and *Backpacker* magazines. *Prevention* identified the Superior Hiking Trail as one of the twelve best trails in the national forests, and *Backpacker* magazine rated it one of the ten best in the country.

Some changes are on the horizon for the Superior Hiking Trail. It is slated to become part of the North Country National Scenic Trail, a 4,500-mile footpath stretching from New York to North Dakota. The Superior Hiking Trail will retain its own identity and will still be maintained and managed by the SHTA, but it will also be a segment of this national trail.

Geology and Scenery along the North Shore

THE DRAMATICALLY BEAUTIFUL LANDSCAPE that we enjoy today along the North Shore is a consequence of a geological history that goes back more than a billion years, into Late Precambrian time.

About 1.1 billion years ago the center of North America began to split apart as slow upwellings in the Earth's plastic mantle (beneath the crust) began to melt, and huge volumes of molten rock called magma leaked up to the surface along fissures in the crust. The present remains of this world-scale crustal feature, known as the Midcontinent Rift System, extend from southeastern Michigan north through its lower and upper peninsulas, westward through Lake Superior, and south-southwest beneath the Twin Cities and Iowa to northeast Kansas. Most of the magma was erupted as great, pancake-like flows of "flood basalt" of a composition similar to the modern or recent eruptions on Hawaii, Iceland, or the Snake River Plain in Idaho. Hundreds of individual lava flows erupted, building up a sequence of layers up to five miles thick along the North Shore area and even thicker along the axis of the rift, now under Lake Superior.

As the crust was pulled apart, the center of the rift gradually subsided, leaving the rock layers tilted on the flanks towards the rift axis. Erosion during the last billion years has etched out these tilted layers to form the "Sawtooth Mountains" in Cook County. These are a series of long ridges with a relatively gentle southeast slope toward Lake Superior and a steep northwest slope, each one sculpted from a single huge lava flow.

Some basaltic magma never made it to the surface, but squeezed between older layers and solidified at various levels in the crust. When magma cools and crystallizes slowly beneath the surface it tends to produce larger crystals, and the rocks thus formed, called intrusive rocks, are generally more resistant when eventually exposed to erosion at the Earth's surface. A very large complex of intrusions, the Duluth Complex, underlies prominent highlands making up central and southwestern Duluth, such as Bardon Peak and Enger Park hill, as well as extending inland northward almost to Ely and eastward into Cook County.

Smaller intrusions, mainly the dark rock diabase, squeezed in at higher levels within the lava-flow sequence. Some of these make up such prominent hills along the North Shore as Hawk Ridge in Duluth, Silver Cliff, most of the rugged highlands between Beaver Bay and Little Marais, Leveaux and Oberg Mountains and the ski hills at Lutsen. Diabase hills continue in the Hovland area and north to the Jackson Lake area.

In some places these diabase magmas carried up huge blocks of a whitish rock called anorthosite, torn loose from the base of the crust about 25 miles beneath the surface. These anorthosites are very resistant to erosion, and now "hold up" such landmarks as Split Rock Lighthouse, Mt. Trudee and other knobs in Tettegouche State Park, and the greatest of all, Carlton Peak by Tofte.

Some of the magma had more silica and less iron than the basaltic magmas, and when it solidified it formed light-colored rocks in contrast to the dark-colored basalt and diabase. Several large rhyolite flows erupted; one of them forms the bold features of Palisade Head and Shovel Point in Lake County. Big rhyolites have also been eroded to form the deep gorges of the Devil Track, Kadunce, and Brule Rivers in Cook County, and of Split Rock River in Lake County.

For some as yet unknown reason, rifting and volcanism ended fairly abruptly without the continent coming completely apart to form a new ocean basin. The rift continued to sink for awhile, however, and streams washed sand, pebbles and mud into the slowly subsiding basin. Several miles of such sediment accumulated in the middle, some of which can be seen today as sandstone on the Bayfield Peninsula and Apostle Islands, Wisconsin. But there was still no Lake Superior.

The last chapter in the saga of the North Shore's landscape was the Great Ice Age. Several times during the last two million years or so (most recently only about 14,000 years ago) great continental glaciers, up to one or two miles thick, built up and oozed southward from Canada. The great ice streams mainly eroded the underlying rock, which had become deeply weathered over the billion years since the time of rifting. The ice found the sedimentary rocks in the middle of the old Midcontinent Rift System to be relatively easy to erode, and it excavated what was to be the Lake Superior basin well below sea level. As the glacier melted back about 11,000 years ago, it uncovered this great scooped-out depression, which of course filled with water. Early stages (such as Glacial Lake Duluth) were several hundred feet higher than the present lake because the ice was still blocking the outlet at the east end. Look for rounded beach stones along the trail, high above the current shoreline. By about 5,000 years ago, Lake Superior as we know it today was well established. Since glaciation, the forests have covered the land, the North Shore streams have been eroding their gorges, and waves have been making beaches and eating away at the shore cliffs and bluffs.

Habitats of the
Superior Hiking Trail

THE SUPERIOR HIKING TRAIL FOLLOWS a corridor that is long enough to have members of three general vegetational groups along its length. One of these is the northern hardwood forest that is at the northwestern limit of its distribution. These northern hardwoods, such as sugar maple, basswood, and oak, are concentrated in the highlands that form the setting for so much of the SHT. This group becomes less common as one travels northeastward from Duluth, and some species disappear completely by Cook County. The second group includes boreal species, like paper birch, balsam fir, and white spruce, which range across northern Minnesota. As the northern hardwoods thin out to the northeast, this second group becomes more prevalent along the SHT. The third group, the Great Lakes/St. Lawrence forest, consists of species found primarily to the east from the Great Lakes to the St. Lawrence lowland, but not ranging far to the north or south. The eastern white pine exemplifies this forest group.

Members of each of these forest groups exist side-by-side in a wide variety of different plant communities. By understanding where a tree comes from geographically, you can begin to make sense of why it is found in particular parts of the SHT. For example, you will find white spruce often in dark, cool valleys that better resemble northern habitat than the warmer, drier ridge tops. Glaciers deposited the rare deep soil along some of the ridges, providing a soil and a habitat for maples quite similar to that found in states further to the south.

The Northern Hardwood Group

Sugar maple is typically the most common tree in the northern hardwoods. Like many others in this group, it is associated with upper slopes, which are less frosty in the late spring. Sugar maple stands occur in all segments of the SHT. Sugar maple forests make fall hikes on the SHT glorious, turning hillsides into gold and red. Sugar maples can be identified by their leaves, whose well-known shape is seen on the Canadian flag.

Northern red oak is another northern hardwood. It is a large tree found at the southwest end of the SHT. However, at the end of its range near the Lake/Cook County line, the oak is a small tree on rocky knobs. Its deep maroon leaves are among the last to drop in the fall.

Yellow birch can grow to the greatest diameter of any of the northern hardwoods. It may be identified in all seasons by scraping the bark from a twig and sniffing for the distinctive odor of wintergreen. These trees sometimes begin life on a dead log, which later rots away to leave a yellow birch growing "on stilts." This species often develops a hollow trunk, and so is an important site for animal denning or nesting.

Other less common members of this group include basswood, ironwood (hop hornbeam), American elm, and mountain maple.

The Boreal Forest Group

Paper birch is extremely common throughout all but wet ground along the SHT. Its white bark and black twigs are more distinctive than its rather plain leaves. This tree requires sunny conditions for growth and fades from the scene as forest stands age and shade the forest floor. Droughts in the late 1980s have led to an extensive dieback of this species, especially near roads and clearcuts.

Balsam fir is a common tree in all parts of the SHT corridor. It seldom achieves great age or size before a storm knocks it down or spruce budworm kills it. Its needles are "flat and flexible," which distinguishes it from the "spiky and sharp" needles of the spruce. Crushing these needles will bring out an aroma reminiscent of winter holidays.

White spruce thrives throughout the SHT corridor where soils are deep enough. You can roll its needles between two fingers, and its bark is rougher than the balsam fir's bark. Large individuals are found here and there. On rock outcrops or in bogs, you may see black spruce, a smaller species. Black spruce is otherwise uncommon because of the scarcity of bogs near Lake Superior.

Balsam poplar is found predominantly in wet soil near streams. The long, sticky aromatic buds are distinctive and perfume the woods during leaf-out in the spring.

Jack pine is scarce along the North Shore in general. The damp summer and lack of expanses of coarse or shallow soils curtail the frequency of the fires on which this species depends.

The Great Lakes/St. Lawrence Group
Several species have their ranges centered in the Great Lakes-St. Lawrence River lowland to the east of Lake Superior. They overlap about equally with the northern portion of the hardwoods and the southern portion of the boreal forest.

Among these species is white pine. White pine is a distinctively majestic tree, with its feathery branches and dark trunk. On closer examination, you'll find that the needles come in clumps of five, as opposed to clumps of two with the red pine. This species was abundant over much of the North Shore region prior to logging. If you see a large, rotting stump on your hike, it is likely the remnant of a white pine that fell to the lumberjacks. The North Shore has a climate that is extremely favorable for the white pine blister rust fungus, so efforts to replant this species have been less successful here than in many other former pineries.

White cedar is common on both wet streams and dry rock outcrops, but only occasional on deep, well-drained soils. What these seemingly contradictory habitats have in common is a lower frequency of fire. White cedar, wherever you find it, is an important winter food for deer. You can identify this tree by its broad, flat, scaly needles and its stringy bark.

Other Trees
Red pine grows in scattered groves, often associated with rock outcrops. Like white pine, it was more abundant before the logging era, though not as common as its five-needled cousin. Disease does not currently pose a great threat to this species, which is also known as "Norway pine" and is the state tree of Minnesota.

Black ash is found mostly in damp ground, rarely with hardwoods on the uplands. It is abundant near many streams. It is the last to leaf out and the first to drop its leaves.

Heartleaf birch is a little-known tree that barely enters the North Shore from the east. It resembles paper birch but has a rosy tinge to its bark. Also, it tends to have branches farther down the trunk than does paper birch, as heartleaf birch is more tolerant of shade. Despite the name, leaf shape is not easy to use for identification. In fact, some botanists list this as a variety of paper birch.

Quaking aspen, also known as "popple" or "poplar," fits into all of the above groups and is one of the most common trees on the SHT. This species occupies more territory than any other North American tree, being found well to the north, south, east and west (with a hiatus in the Great Plains). It can be expected in the trail corridor wherever there are younger forests on deep soils. Old, shady stands are unlikely to have much aspen, although large trembling aspen are found in some places. This species increased greatly as the land was opened up by lumbering for pine and by the fires that sometimes followed.

Plants

The diversity of tree types parallels a diversity of wildflowers and other herbaceous growth. Minor variations in soil types can lead to major changes in the flora on the forest floor. Some stretches of rich soil will be covered with large-leaf aster and bluebead lily, while bare granitic rock may support some caribou moss and the polypody fern. Each month of spring, summer, and fall brings a new range of color and growth. As the snow melts in spring, look for violets, marsh marigold and wild lily-of-the-valley. As summer nears, the moccasin flowers and ladyslippers bloom, often in isolated and hard-to-find patches. In the heat of summer, watch for columbine, wild roses, buttercup and the towering cow parsnip. The onset of fall brings the asters and the goldenrods, which can bloom well into October.

Other flowers grow in distinct habitats, such as the water lilies and cattails in marshes; labrador tea, pitcher plant, and bog laurel in bogs; and twinflower, wintergreen and indian pipe in pine duff.

Overall, let these clues of trees and flowers reflect the varied terrain through which the SHT passes. On any given section of the trail you will pass through three, four or a dozen different habitats. Landforms, microclimates and succession determined these habitats, and the trees and other plants tell you fascinating stories about survival, and thriving, in the north woods.

Wildflower Calendar for the Superior Hiking Trail

May

Bloodroot	Sanguinaria canadensis
Violets	Viola
Wild Lily-of-the-Valley	Maianthemum canadense
Common Strawberry	Fuagaria virginiana
Marsh-marigold	Caltha palustris
Spring Beauty	Claytonia virginica
Wood Anemone	Anemone quinquefolia
Goldthread	Coptis groenlandica

June

Nodding Trillium	Trillium cernuum
Starflower	Trientalis borealis
Bunchberry	Cornus canadensis
Columbine	Aquilegia canadensis
Moccasin Flower	Cypripedium acaule
Larger Blue-flag	Iris versicolor
Blue-bead Lily	Clintonia borealis

July

Meadowsweet	Spiraea latifolia
Spreading Dogbane	Apocynum androsaemifolium
Northern Bedstraw	Galium boreale
Indian-pipe	Monotropa uniflora
Heal-all	Prunella vulgaris
Cow-parsnip	Heracleum maximum

August

Goldenrods	Solidago
Large-leaf Aster	Aster macrophyllus
Fireweed	Epilobium angustifolium
Jewelweed	Impatiens capensis
Evening Primrose	Oenothera
Spotted Joe-Pye-Weed	Eupatorium maculatum

Birds of the
Lake Superior Highlands

O NE OF THE GREAT PLEASURES in walking through the woods is being attuned to what other creatures inhabit the same area. Most forest creatures are wary and their presence is not easily revealed. Birds, because they fly and they sing while nesting, are more conspicuous than most other vertebrates and thus add a dimension to the hike, whether you are teasing out a scolding ovenbird from the undergrowth or watching hawks migrate in the fall from one of the many overlooks.

The type of bird watching you may experience along the Superior Hiking Trail depends on the character of the woods, the season of the year and the weather. Gulls, sea ducks, and out-of-range migrants are seen on Lake Superior, and the SHT has opened up a path into the forest that brings the hiker closer to the birds that inhabit the hills back from the shore. One can hike, look and listen for some of the approximately 100 species of birds that breed in summer in the Lake Superior Highlands, which is the ecoregion made up of the topography, climate, soils and vegetation that the SHT traverses.

From Jay Cooke State Park, along the ridgeline above Duluth and through the Lake Superior Highlands, a mixture of deciduous and coniferous types of vegetation exists. Habitat for birds is almost entirely determined by the vegetation. Openings, either woodland ponds and streams, brushlands or cutovers, as well as an occasional boreal conifer bog or open ledge, provide variety.

The greatest portion of the species present along the SHT, about three fourths, are upland forest inhabitants, most of which are there for only for a short period of time during the breeding season (early May to early August). At least 73 species probably nest in these uplands. A very few of these birds are permanent residents and might be found in winter woods on a snowshoe trek. The rest are here in the summer to take advantage of the abundant insects (mostly caterpillars) to feed their young, and the many diverse habitats provided by the mixed forest.

The summer hiker who is not a birder is probably amazed that the woods contain so many species. Except for the dawn chorus (starting from 4:30 a.m. when even a dedicated nature explorer is likely trying to sleep), their presence is revealed only by scolding chips or an occasional burst of song. To really appreciate the birds along the SHT, learning the songs, at least of some of the common species, will add pleasure to the hiking experience. The intense singing period is at the height of the nesting cycle. The best way to learn the songs is spotting the songster with binoculars and identifying it while it sings.

Weather is always a variable in birdwatching. The fall days with a good northwest wind, following the passage

Birds of Ponds and Streams

- great blue heron
- wood duck
- mallard
- blue-winged teal
- ring-necked duck
- common goldeneye
- hooded merganser
- spotted sandpiper
- belted kingfisher
- tree swallow

Birds of Lowland Conifers

- olive-sided flycatcher
- yellow-bellied flycatcher
- gray jay
- boreal chickadee
- Connecticut warbler
- Lincoln's sparrow

Birds of Shrub Wetlands

- American woodcock
- alder flycatcher
- gray catbird
- golden-winged warbler
- Tennessee warbler
- yellow warbler
- northern waterthrush
- common yellowthroat
- Wilson's warbler
- swamp sparrow

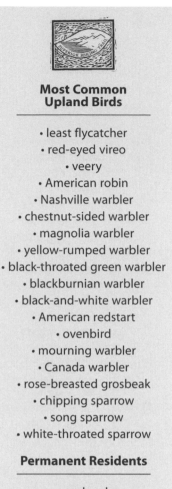

Most Common Upland Birds

- least flycatcher
- red-eyed vireo
- veery
- American robin
- Nashville warbler
- chestnut-sided warbler
- magnolia warbler
- yellow-rumped warbler
- black-throated green warbler
- blackburnian warbler
- black-and-white warbler
- American redstart
- ovenbird
- mourning warbler
- Canada warbler
- rose-breasted grosbeak
- chipping sparrow
- song sparrow
- white-throated sparrow

Permanent Residents

- goshawk
- ruffed grouse
- spruce grouse
- great horned owl
- barred owl
- downy woodpecker
- hairy woodpecker
- pileated woodpecker
- blue jay
- common raven
- black-capped chickadee
- red-breasted nuthatch

of a cold front, bring rewarding hawk-watching. Raptors and other day-time migrants are funneled along the shore of Lake Superior and use the updrafts from the hills to aid them in their flight. The bulk of the hawk migration is from about the 10th of September through the 10th of October, but eagles and other northern raptors can be seen through early December. The overlooks along the SHT provide opportunities for witnessing this migration. The highest concentrations are near Duluth; a SHT spur takes hikers to Hawk Ridge, one of the famous hawk-watching spots in the United States. Other birds migrate in flocks and can be seen in numbers along the North Shore: blue jay, American crow, common raven, American robin, cedar waxwing, and seven species of winter finches. Flocks of small birds may be spotted feeding in the treetops.

Each hiking trip, depending on the time and place, can produce a different experience with the birds in the woods. Storing up these moments expands the memory of the event and can also add to the knowledge of the birds of the Superior Hiking Trail.

Animals of the Superior Hiking Trail

DESCRIBING THE ANIMAL LIFE of the North Shore and the Superior Hiking Trail is challenging because of its great variety. Fortunately, for the sake of brevity, it's possible to make some distinctions. First of all, there are animals in the official sense, that is, things that move and eat other things. But then there are "animals," generally fuzzy things with one set of eyes. Is that black fly biting your earlobe an animal? Yes, indeed. But a lot of people would rather swat the black fly while looking for a "real" animal like a deer, wolf, or turtle. Insects, reptiles, fish, and amphibians are all animals but, due to space, will receive only short notice here. The birds of the SHT are covered in the previous chapter. This chapter will mostly cover the mammals of the SHT.

As you hike, you may encounter animals of three basic types:

1) Small animals that are common but seldom seen;

2) Animals that are somewhat common and often seen; and

3) Medium to large, generally carnivorous animals that are rare, wide-ranging and also seldom seen.

On your typical day hike you probably won't see a lot of animals besides birds and insects. That's not because they aren't there. But unless you have the eyes of a hawk, you'll likely miss the mice and shrews that cruise the underbrush. And unless you are quiet and lucky, you probably won't see a wolf. However, white-tail deer, snowshoe hare and red squirrel, among others, are animals that are commonly seen along the SHT.

Although you may not see any large mammal, you will undoubtedly see some evidence of their passing. They are out there. Many mammals are active during the morning and evenings, but rest during the day. The white-tail deer you see bounding through the forest may have been resting from a busy night of feeding before you startled it. If you want to learn about the animals of the SHT, you will do better to look for evidence rather than the animal itself.

If you do look for animal signs, you won't be disappointed. In a muddy section of the SHT, look for tracks of deer, moose and wolves, animals likely to use the SHT as an easy path through remote woods. Scat (animal feces) is another obvious sign, and it becomes more obvious when an animal uses scat to mark territory. When there is a prominent, bare rock near the trail, look for wolf or coyote scat (told by the ropy texture, hair and bone chip content) or that of the fisher or marten (which is long, slender, and dark). All these mammals use scat to mark their territory with both its sight and smell. Other signs of large animals include bark rubbings by male moose and deer, deer and moose beds in grassy areas, and nests. If this sort of animal watching interests you, bring a book such as Peterson's *A Field Guide to Animal Tracks*. There are some fascinating stories to be read in the woods.

Small Animals that are Common but Seldom Seen

This category includes all the shrews, voles, mice, and little weasels. These animals are used to fleeing at the sound (or feel) of danger. You'll see their trails crossing above or sometimes below the SHT. In open areas, look for the birds like kestrels that are looking, in turn, for these little creatures. At dusk, in a campsite, a woodland deer mouse or short-tailed shrew might try to get into your food or clean up your dinner scraps.

These small creatures play important roles in ecosystems as primary consumers and carnivores (mostly of insects). They also aerate and enrich the soil with their tunnels. For every one large, dramatic carnivore in the food web there are thousands of little creatures, all doing their part to keep the cycles flowing. And in case you are fortunate enough to encounter one, remember that the short-tailed shrew is one of only two North American mammals with a venomous bite.

Animals that are Somewhat Common and Often Seen

White-tail deer. Although the deer is a common resident now, a century ago there were hardly any here. Instead there were woodland caribou, which thrived on lichens and moss of the primordial forest. Now, with logging and other habitat changes, the caribou are only in Canada (with the notable exception of a caribou wandering in Hovland in the winter of 1980-81). Deer congregate along the North Shore in winter and early spring, where snowfall is lighter and melts sooner, making food more accessible and travel easier. The Jonvik deer yard near Lutsen is one of the largest deer yards in the state. For two weeks in the fall, generally the first and second weeks in November, deer are hunted all along the SHT, so wear bright colors.

Moose. Count yourself fortunate if you encounter one of these gentle giants on your hike. You'll increase your luck if you look carefully in the low, wet areas near the SHT. Look for a brown boulder moving among the lily pads. In general, deer and moose populations do not intermix. The deer carry a flatworm that doesn't harm the deer but is fatal to the moose. Moose droppings are thumb-size, light brown pellets, found in large piles. Moose tracks have the same double half-moon shape of the deer, but are at least twice as long. Some classic moose habitat along the SHT includes Jonvik Creek and the wetlands around Grand Portage.

Black bear. The black bear is an incredible survivor. It uses every trick in the book to survive the north woods. Bears have one of the most diverse natural diets around, including your food bag if you're not careful. Bears' diet follows the season: when the blueberries are ripe, they gorge on blueberries, and likewise with the hazelnuts or other edibles. When there's no more fresh food, around the end of September, bears begin to go into torpor, a sort of intermittent hibernation. The SHT passes near a grove of oak trees in Tettegouche State Park that is a magnet for bears from 50 miles around when the acorns are ripe in the fall. Treat these creatures with the respect they deserve—that includes putting your food far out of reach when you're camping.

Weasels. You may not see a weasel, but weasels are mammals worth noting. There is a whole family of weasels of all different sizes, all with the same mode of survival: chase and kill. The short-tailed weasel, or ermine, chases mice; the fisher and marten chase larger prey such as squirrels and hares. You'll be thrilled if you ever witness one of their chases. In the winter, look for their distinctive bounding tracks in the snow.

Snowshoe hare. Depending on their population cycles, you may see lots of hares or you may see none. Even if they are around, you have to look carefully. With their changing coat, they are always well camouflaged. They prefer thickets of shrubs and short trees, which give them plenty of cover from predators such as great-horned owls and lynx.

Red squirrel. The sound of a red squirrel defending its territory is one of the standard anthems of the north woods. That sharp, rattling "chirrrr" is the squirrel's way of telling you to beat it. Each squirrel defends a territory of about a 200-yard diameter circle. If the summer and fall harvests are good, the squirrel will store up to 14,000 food items in this territory, including cones, mushrooms and nuts (the mushrooms are hung on tree bark where they can dry). Red squirrels can become overly friendly in campsites if they are fed by hikers.

Beaver. As the SHT works its way up and down hills and across streams, it is bound to take you through the work of the beaver. Sometimes, though, you won't even notice. The beaver, with its propensity to change the environment to suit its needs (like another mammal, *Homo sapiens)*, has been around long enough that its ponds have turned into forests. Some particularly spectacular beaver ponds can be found near Sawmill Creek and on Jonvik Creek, where the SHT crosses the creek on a beaver dam, as well as along the upper reaches of the Gooseberry River.

Fox. The red fox shows several color variations from red to black, dark brown, and even silver. It has white undersides with black legs and a white tip on the trail. It can be found in open fields near woodlands.

Medium-to-Large, Generally Carnivorous Animals that are Rare, Wide-Ranging and also Seldom Seen

Timber wolf. Along the North Shore, starting northeast of Two Harbors, there are numerous packs of wolves. This is, however, the fringe of their population. The traffic and development of Highway 61 keeps most wolves inland, though the SHT is in some prime wolf territory. Look for scat and tracks along the SHT, and also the occasional kill site of a well-broken-up deer carcass. The presence of the wolves is a testimony to the wildness of the land through which you are traveling.

Coyote. Where there aren't wolves along the North Shore, there are likely to be coyotes. Wolves defend their territories from coyotes, but as the edge of wolf range fluctuates, so does the coyote range. Coyotes are smaller than wolves but larger than foxes and can be identified by their large ears and bouncing gait. They're more of a "suburban" animal, more accustomed to human presence. Like wolves, they have eerie, though distinct, howling sessions.

Lynx, bobcat, and mountain lion. Solitary hunters, these wild cats prey mostly on the snowshoe hare, and so their populations vary with the hare's. The bobcat is at the northern edge of its range and the lynx is at its southern edge. The lynx travels 3–6 miles a night in search of food, but success is less than fifty-fifty each night. Both cats have ranges rather than territories, which means they can overlap with others of the same species and are not generally defended. Another even bigger cat, the mountain lion, has been spotted in recent years in St. Louis and Cook Counties.

Other Animals on the Superior Hiking Trail

Insects are animals, right? If you're out in May through September, you'll likely encounter some of these. Not all of them are out to bite you, either. But some will try. Watch for black flies in May and June, various species of mosquito from May to September, and deer and horse flies in July and August. Look for dragonflies, leeches, colorful beetles, and aquatic insects in the streams. Also in the streams you'll find brook trout, and a host of frogs, turtles, and salamanders.

The animal life along the North Shore is a significant part of what makes the SHT so special. With careful observation, you'll find that there is a world of creatures as wild and dramatic as the cliffs and mountains of the shore. As you wind your way through different habitats, keep an eye out for the "locals." Either a sighting or a sign will let you in on part of the great mystery of this land.

General North Shore History

THE FIRST PEOPLE TO ENTER the North Shore region arrived around 10,000 years ago. These Paleo-Indians entered the region during the final retreat of the Wisconsin Glaciation. As the Superior ice lobe melted back to the northeast, it blocked the present outlet of Lake Superior, causing lake levels to rise above their present level by up to 450 feet.

This enlarged Lake Superior is known as Glacial Lake Duluth, and in many areas the ancient shoreline closely follows the ridgeline that much of the Superior Hiking Trail now follows. The Paleo-Indians were big game hunters of caribou, bison, musk ox, and possibly mammoth. In all probability, these hunters followed the shoreline of this lake of glacial meltwater along these present-day ridge tops.

The Old Copper Culture followed the Paleo-Indian cultural tradition around Lake Superior and existed from about 5,000 years ago until about 2,000 years ago. During this time the Indians used raw native copper, found on Isle Royale and in northern Michigan, hammering it into tools. Occasionally copper artifacts, in the form of spear points, knives, and fish hooks, are found along the North Shore. If you find copper or stone tools, contact one of the state parks. These finds are very rare and the information will add to the knowledge of this early history.

Many waves of Indian people inhabited the North Shore prior to European contact. The first Europeans, French explorers and fur traders, reached the Lake Superior country about 1620. At that time, the Ojibwa (also called Anishinabe or Chippewa) inhabited the eastern end of the lake as far west as the Upper Peninsula of Michigan. Their culture centered at the rapids at the outlet of the big lake. By 1650 the French had encountered the Dakota, or Sioux, at the head of the lake. Along the North Shore lived the Assiniboine and the Cree. As the fur trade moved west over the next 100 years, so did the Ojibway, displacing by 1750 the Dakota, the Assiniboine, and the Cree, who moved farther to the west and north.

By 1780, the Europeans had established fur trading posts at the mouth of the St. Louis River and at Grand Portage. The Ojibwa were firmly established on the western end of Lake Superior and in northeastern Minnesota. Both Europeans and Ojibwa navigated their frail birch bark canoes along the rugged North Shore between these two important sites of early commerce and, although the Ojibwa did have foot trails heading inland at different points along the shore, the early traders had little reason to leave the lake and explore the adjacent uplands.

In 1854, the Ojibwa signed the Treaty of La Pointe, which opened up northeastern Minnesota to mineral exploration and settlement. The first permanent settlement was a group of Germans from Ohio who settled at Beaver Bay in 1856. The late 1800s saw a rise of commercial herring fishing along the North Shore and settlement by Scandinavian immigrants. It was said that nearly every cove harbored at least one fisherman's shanty.

Across Lake Superior, Michigan lumber barons had cut most of the big stands of virgin white pine in Michigan by 1890. They then set their sights on Lake Superior's North Shore. Between 1890 and 1910, millions of board feet of red and white pine were cut from the hills along the North Shore. Temporary railroads transported the logs down to Lake Superior where they were rafted up and towed by tugboat to sawmills in Duluth, Superior, Bayfield, and Ashland. Today many of these old railroad grades—most used only for one or two seasons—are still visible. In places, the SHT either crosses or follows some of these straight and level grades such as the Alger, Nestor and Merrill-Ring grades.

Since northeastern Minnesota was opened to exploration, mining has had an active history on the North Shore. Small, unproductive copper explorations began along some of the rivers in the 1850s and 1860s.

Beginning in 1884, high-grade iron ore from the Iron Range in north-eastern Minnesota was shipped from the huge ore docks in Two Harbors on ore boats bound for the mills on the lower Great Lakes.

At the turn of the century a new company was formed in Two Harbors, Minnesota Mining and Manufacturing. Known today as 3M, the company planned to mine an abrasive rock, misidentified as corundum, at Crystal Bay near the mouth of the Baptism River. At the same time, the North Shore Abrasives Company was formed to mine the same type of rock from a location near Split Rock. In both cases the rock was found to be too soft to serve as an abrasive, and mining operations were discontinued by 1906.

Taconite pellets, refined from low-grade taconite iron ore, were first produced in the mid-1950s from mines on the Mesabi Iron Range. Taconite pellets continue to be processed and shipped to steel plants on the lower Great Lakes from Duluth, Two Harbors, and Silver Bay. Operational railroad tracks crossed by the SHT connect the mines near Ely, Babbitt and Hoyt Lakes with these shipping points along the North Shore.

It is obvious to anyone visiting the North Shore that tourism and recreation have had, and continue to have, a major impact on local development. As early as 1910, when Split Rock Lighthouse was built, the lightkeeper recorded that tourists began visiting the light station by sailboat. Even though a one-lane wagon road was built between certain points along the shore in the 1890s, the present North Shore highway was not completed between Duluth and the Canadian border until 1924. When the highway was completed, camping and cabin resorts sprang up along the shore. Seven state parks were set aside and protected, joined most recently by the eighth, Grand Portage State Park. Today, hikers on the SHT can still look upon many of the same unspoiled vistas that the Native Americans and the first French explorers saw.

For more information on the cultures and peoples that have inhabited the North Shore, visit the Cook County Historical Society, the Lake County Historical Society, or the Split Rock Lighthouse Visitor Center.

Backpacking on the Superior Hiking Trail

BACKPACKING ALLOWS YOU TO experience the Superior Hiking Trail intimately and up close. While this chapter will help hikers enjoy the trail more fully, experience is the best teacher. Also, please be sure to read the next chapter on minimum impact trail use and "Leave No Trace" principles. Using these principles will help protect the SHT for future generations.

There are 86 backcountry campsites located about every five to ten miles along the SHT, except in the Duluth section. There are no reservations, fees, or permits required to use the campsites. Since the SHT crosses so much private land and state park land and oftentimes land ownership is not marked, campers must camp only at designated campsites. Each campsite has two to eight tent pads (a tent pad is a level area on natural soil), a fire ring, and a backcountry latrine. Some of the campsites are called "multi-group" campsites and are designed for larger groups, but any party can camp at any campsite. Parties are required to share campsites. All parties need to share the one established campfire ring and not make additional fire rings, since the soil under a fire ring must be dug out to at least two feet to remove any roots that could catch on fire. In the trail section chapters, each campsite is described. Information includes the number of tent pads, the water source for the campsite, and the distance to the previous and next campsites. This information is invaluable for planning your trip. It is a good idea to carry the guidebook or photocopies of the sections you are hiking. It can be particularly useful if your trip doesn't go according to plan, as sometimes happens, and you need to figure out an alternative campsite.

Only surface water is available along the SHT. All drinking water must be boiled, filtered or chemically treated. Most campsites have a stream, river, pond or lake as their water source. Please note that campsite water sources that are small creeks may be dry by the end of the summer and water must be obtained before reaching the campsite. The campsite description details whether the water source may be unreliable in dry weather conditions. When the water source is from a beaver pond, it's a good idea to strain the water through a bandana or something similar before treating to remove any organic matter that can clog a filter or cause water purification tablets not to work as effectively.

Always hang your food, garbage, and any items that have a smell in a bag at night or when away from your campsite. Bags should be at least ten feet off the ground and five feet away from a tree trunk. Bears do not associate the SHT campsites with food and are rarely a problem on the trail, but that's because hikers do a good job of hanging their food and keeping a clean campsite.

General Backpacking Information

It is always a good idea to let someone know your plans. Tell someone where you plan to hike and when you plan to arrive; then check in when you return. The SHT is not patrolled, so your safety or rescue in an emergency may depend on this common-sense precaution. All three counties the SHT travels through—St. Louis, Lake, and Cook Counties—have Search and Rescue units that can be called using the 911 system. Be aware, however, that cell phone reception is not available in all areas on the SHT.

Each section on the SHT begins and ends at a trailhead parking lot. Each section chapter describes the parking and whether overnight parking is okay. In general, you can park overnight at most SHT parking lots for as long as you like, with some exceptions. If the trailhead parking lot is in a state park, you can park overnight for as long as you want with a state park sticker. State park staff will direct you where to park for overnight parking.

Always carry a map of your route when you hike. Even though the SHT is paint blazed, there are plenty of other trails, roads, and game trails that cross the SHT to cause confusion at times. The SHTA sells this guidebook as well as pocket maps for each section. Follow along in the guidebook or pocket map so that if you have lost the trail or if you need to leave the trail for an emergency, you'll have a good idea of your location. It's also a good idea to carry a compass and know how to use it.

Through-Hiking the Superior Hiking Trail

Up to 200 people through-hike the SHT each year. The length of a through-hike from Fox Farm Road, East Trailhead through Otter Lake Road is 275 miles. The average time to through-hike the trail is about three to four weeks, with an average distance of about ten miles a day. This guidebook is written from the south end of the trail to the north end, but all mileages from north to south are noted as well. If you have two vehicles you can hike in either direction. Most backpackers with only one vehicle tend to hike from north to south because it is easier to get a ride to the remote northern end and then hike south to the more developed end. There is no cell phone reception at the north end of the trail.

The Superior Shuttle services the entire trail from Fox Farm/East Trailhead to Otter Lake Road. There are some trailheads you can go to or be picked up from only with an advance reservation so be sure to check the schedule closely when doing your planning. There are bus and taxi services available in Duluth.

To re-supply with food and other items, you can mail packages to post offices close to the SHT. The address is: Your Name, c/o General Delivery, Town, State, Zip. The package will be held for 30 days from the date of delivery. It can be helpful to write "Hold for SHT Hiker" on the package. You can also purchase supplies from local grocery stores. Below is a chart of towns within two to four miles of the SHT. The chart lists the services available at each town and an approximate distance from the trailhead to the town.

North Shore Community	Post Office Zip Code	Services Available	Medical Available	Miles to Town
Duluth	55806 Main Post Office	M, L, G, C, LM, O	Hospital (2) Clinics	In town
Two Harbors	55616	M, L, G, C, LM, O	Hospital	6.0
Beaver Bay	55601	M, L, LG, LM	—	1.5
Silver Bay	55614	M, L, G, LM, C	Clinic	2.5
Finland	55603	M, L, G, C	—	1.3
Schroeder	55613	L, C	—	2.4
Tofte	55615	M, L, G, O	—	2.7
Lutsen Mtns. Rec Area	55612	M, L, LG	—	0.3
Lutsen Post Office (via Caribou Trail)	55612	G	—	4.5
Grand Marais	55604	M, L, G, C, LM, O	Hospital	2.5
Hovland	55606	M, LG	—	3.5

Services Key
M = meals
L = lodging
G = groceries
LG = limited groceries
C = camping
LM = laundromat
O = outfitting supplies

Another way to re-supply is through the Superior Shuttle. The Shuttle can deliver a package to you at a specified trailhead on a specific date. The state parks do not hold packages for hikers.

There are many good resources available that detail what equipment and clothing to take when backpacking. The sport has changed significantly in the last ten years with new lightweight gear and other innovations being developed all the time. In general, be aware that the weather near Lake Superior is unpredictable and thunderstorms or cold weather can blow in unexpectedly. It is also colder than you might expect at night, even in summer. Always carry rain gear and warm clothing with you.

The worst month for biting insects is June. Ticks can also be a problem. Wood ticks generally do not cause disease but deer ticks, which are about the size of a sesame seed and can cause Lyme Disease, are increasing in the southern part of the SHT, although reported cases of Lyme Disease are rare. It's a good idea to take insect repellant and possibly a headnet with you. Also do a "tick check" each night. Consider pre-treating your clothing with a tick spray containing permethrin. Usually by July insects are at a tolerable level, although they will still be around until they are killed by frost, usually in late September.

Minimum Impact Trail Use: Leave No Trace

AS MORE AND MORE HIKERS and backpackers use the Superior Hiking Trail, minimizing impacts is crucial to protecting the trail and the natural environment of the trail. The Superior Hiking Trail Association supports a set of principles called the Leave No Trace principles and encourages all trail users to follow them. These guidelines are in place to help protect the environment and a high quality hiking experience. Below are guidelines adapted for the Superior Hiking Trail:

Plan ahead and prepare. Know the type of terrain and the range of weather conditions you might encounter. Be prepared for any emergencies you might encounter. Always use a map when hiking on the trail. Know and respect the rules for the trail.

Travel and camp on durable surfaces. Use the existing main trail and spur trails. Stay on the trail at all times on signed private lands and in signed sensitive areas. Always walk single file and avoid shortcuts to avoid damage to the trail and surrounding area. Walk through mud puddles to avoid widening the trail. Never blaze trees or use other markers.

Use the designated campsites and plan your trip mileage to use designated campsites. Camping at the campsites is on a first-come, first-use basis. Parties are asked to share campsites if tent pads are available.

Camping is absolutely prohibited on private lands and in state parks. Use the tent pads that have been cleared and do not make new ones. Do not trench around the tent.

Dispose of waste properly. Pack it in, pack it out. Pack out all trash, leftover food, and litter. Inspect your campsite and rest areas for trash or spilled foods. Seal all waste in airtight containers and hang it with your food bag each night. Pick up trash others have left. Never bury garbage.

Use the latrines located at each campsite and dispose of toilet paper only in the latrines. Pack out all sanitary products. If you aren't near a latrine, dig a small hole for human waste 3-6 inches deep at least 200 feet from a water source. Fill it in and camouflage when finished.

Never use soap in a lake or stream—carry water 200 feet from water sources to wash dishes or yourself. Dispose of dishwater well away from a water source and from your campsite.

Leave what you find. Leave rocks, plants and other natural objects as you find them. Do not touch or take cultural or historic structures or artifacts.

Minimize campfire impacts. Use a lightweight stove for cooking and enjoy a small candle lantern for light. If you make a fire, make it only in the fire ring provided at each campsite. If you are sharing the campsite with another party, do not build a second fire. Burn only small diameter wood found on the ground. Do not damage live trees. Never take birch bark from trees. Be sure your campfire is completely out before you leave camp.

Respect wildlife. Observe wildlife from a distance. Do not try to attract or approach wild animals. Never feed animals human food. This disrupts their natural food cycle. Pets must be on leash at all times to avoid disturbing wildlife. Always hang your food and garbage (or keep in a bear-proof container) at night or when away from your campsite to avoid attracting wildlife.

Be considerate of other visitors. Respect other visitors and protect the quality of their experience. Yield to other users on the trail. Let nature's sounds prevail. Avoid loud voices and noises. Be courteous when sharing a campsite with another party.

The Best of the
Superior Hiking Trail

EVERY SECTION OF THE Superior Hiking Trail is the
best...for some reason. Over the years, some sections have
become better known than others. People have voted with their
feet for favorites like Oberg Mountain in the fall. Here are suggestions
for your hiking selection.

Crowd Favorites

These sections are scenic and easy to reach. They are popular for good
reason. Be prepared for great hiking and a few other folks along the trail.
Some of these hikes are loops and some of them are out-and-back hikes.

• **Split Rock River Loop:** Up and down the banks of this spirited
river (5.0 miles, see page 107).

• **Bean and Bear Lakes Loop** (also called the Twin Lakes Trail):
Climb to a mountainous setting and enjoy the scenic lakes below (6.6
or 7.6 mile loops, see page 121).

• **Mount Trudee:** A challenging uphill climb to spectacular views
in Tettegouche State Park (4.8 miles one-way from Tettegouche, see
page 121).

• **Carlton Peak:** A steep climb to one of the highest mountains in
Minnesota (3.1 miles one-way from Temperance River, 1.7 miles one-
way from Sawbill Trail, see page 160).

• **Oberg Mountain Loop:** A great meander to scenic views, especially in fall colors (1.8 mile loop, see page 167 and page 171).

• **Cascade River:** Go up one side of the river to Co. Rd. 45 and return on the other (7.8 miles, see page 182).

• **Cove Point Loop:** The spur trail goes from Cove Point Lodge up to the radio tower, then makes a scenic loop along Fault Line Ridge and returns to the lodge (6.0 miles, see page 116).

Wilderness Treks

Long-distance sections with fewer people along the trail.
• Split Rock to Beaver Bay
• Finland Recreation Center to Crosby-Manitou State Park
• Crosby-Manitou State Park to Caribou River
• Cascade River State Park to Bally Creek Rd.
• Jackson Lake Rd. to Otter Lake Rd.

Scenic Shorties

Shorter walks to scenic spots.
• Wolf Rock from Castle Danger trailhead (0.5 miles one-way, see page 98).
• Hwy. 1 to Fantasia overlooks (1.4 miles one-way, see page 129).
• Lake Co. Rd. 6 to Section 13 cliffs (1.3 miles one-way, see page 133).
• Cook Co. Rd. 58 to Devil Track River (2.5 miles one-way, see page 193).
• Kadunce River (0.7 miles one-way, see page 202).

Best Trout Fishing

Cross the river on a scenic bridge and toss a lure.
• Gooseberry River
• Split Rock River
• Manitou River
• Cascade River
• Poplar River

Most Dramatic Peaks

• Ely's Peak
• Mount Trudee
• Carlton Peak
• Oberg Mountain
• Pincushion Mountain

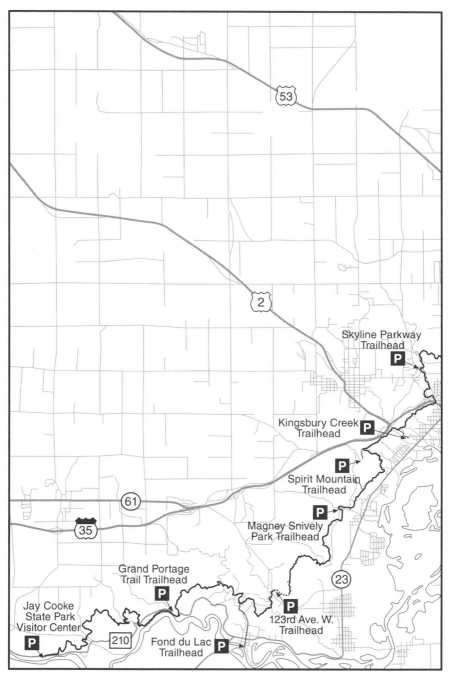

Duluth Area Locator Map

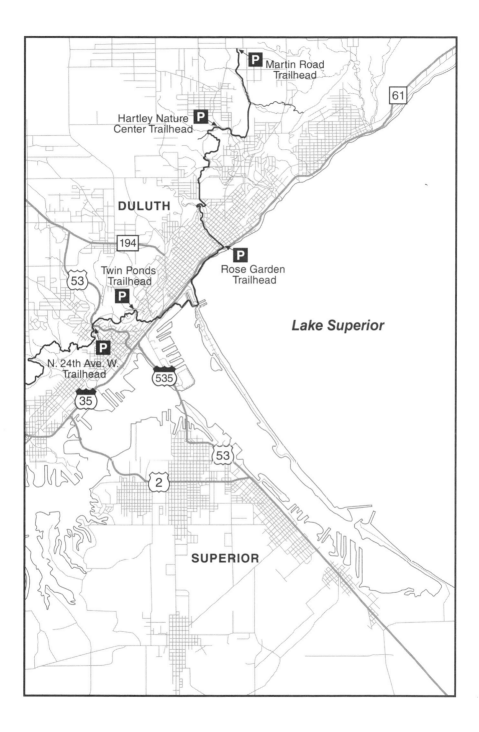

P Martin Road
Trailhead

61

Hartley Nature P
Center Trailhead

DULUTH

194

Rose Garden
Trailhead

P

53

Twin Ponds
Trailhead

P

Lake Superior

N. 24th Ave. W.
Trailhead

P

535

35

53

2

SUPERIOR

Map & Trail Description Information

North is always to the top of the page. The SHT runs primarily in a SW to NE direction.

Scale 1" = 1 Mile.

Trail mileage. For each paragraph, the first number gives the mileage from the beginning trailhead. The number in parentheses is for hiking the section from the ending trailhead.

Trail marking. The SHT main trail is paint blazed with blue rectangles. Spur trails and overlook trails are marked with white rectangles. Two rectangles side by side indicate a sharp turn in the trail. The higher blaze shows the direction the trail turns.

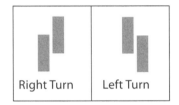

| Right Turn | Left Turn |

Map Legend

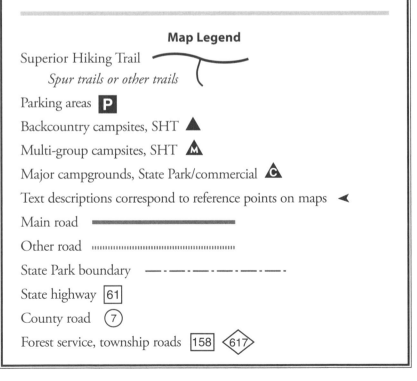

Superior Hiking Trail

Spur trails or other trails

Parking areas **P**

Backcountry campsites, SHT ▲

Multi-group campsites, SHT ▲ (M)

Major campgrounds, State Park/commercial ▲ (C)

Text descriptions correspond to reference points on maps ◄

Main road ▬▬▬▬▬▬

Other road ▪▪▪▪▪▪▪▪▪▪▪▪▪▪▪▪▪▪▪▪▪▪▪▪▪▪▪

State Park boundary — · — — · — — · — — · —

State highway 61

County road ⑦

Forest service, township roads 158 ◇617◇

Jay Cooke State Park Visitor Center to Jay Cooke State Park Grand Portage Trail Trailhead

6.6 miles

Section description: Jay Cooke State Park Visitor Center on Hwy. 210 to Jay Cooke State Park Grand Portage Trail Trailhead on Hwy. 210

Access and parking: *Directions to beginning trailhead:* 1) From the south: take I-35 Carlton Exit #235 and go right (east) on Hwy. 210 5.5 miles to Jay Cooke State Park Visitor Center. 2) From the north: take I-35 Co. Rd. 1/Thomson/Esko Exit #242. Turn left on Co. Rd. 1 (Thomson Road) and go 3.4 miles to intersection with Hwy. 210. Turn left on Hwy 210 and go 1.6 miles to Visitor Center. State park sticker required. Overnight parking okay.

Facilities at beginning trailhead: park office, picnic building, restrooms, campground

Designated campsites on this section: none (four fee backpack campsites in state park)

Synopsis: This first section of the Superior Hiking Trail shares state park trails through a variety of forest habitats. Highlights include views of the St. Louis River Valley, groves of white pine trees and following the historic portage route along the St. Louis River. A hidden treasure is Gill Creek, nestled at the bottom of a steep creek valley.

Mile-by-Mile Description

0.0 (6.6) Visitor Center parking lot and White Pine Trail

SHT begins from Visitor Center on connector trail north (away from Visitor Center) from parking lot, crosses Hwy. 210, and turns right (east) on White Pine Trail with glimpses of occasional large white pines. Trail rises to view of St. Louis River Valley just before day use hut and soon crosses creek on wide bridge. At intersection with Oldenburg Picnic Area, SHT continues on White Pine Trail by veering left and continuing for another 200 feet to next intersection, with Greely Trail.

(1.4) (5.2) Greely Trail
At intersection with Greely Trail (No. 3), SHT turns right (north) and goes onto Greely Trail. After passing through meadow under powerlines, trail comes to reservoir called Forbay Lake, turns right and follows alongside reservoir until it crosses reservoir on concrete drive next to gatehouse (Note: From the north, this trail crossing is labeled Forbay Trail and Greely Trail). After gatehouse, trail crosses Jay Cooke Rd. diagonally and enters woods again. SHT continues on Greely Trail through older maple-oak forest with occasional large yellow birch.

(2.4) (4.2) First intersection of Greely Trail and Munger Trail
Still following the Greely Trail, SHT comes to paved Munger Trail, turns right (northeast) onto Munger Trail and follows it for 675 feet, passing Hemlock Ravine, a Scientific Natural Area. SHT turns right (southeast) off Munger Trail continuing through woods on Greely Trail. Trail comes again to Munger Trail, turns right and follows Munger Trail for a few feet, then turns right again and goes back into woods still on Greely Trail. Trail turns right for third time onto Munger Trail, goes 325 feet and comes to unmarked right turn by horse trail sign. Watch carefully for this sign. Greely Trail turns right here and goes 20 feet to major trail intersection (No. 15).

(2.9) (3.7) Triangle Trail
At intersection of Greely Trail and Triangle Trail (No. 15), SHT turns right (southeast) onto Triangle Trail and follows Triangle Trail for 0.3 miles. At next major intersection (No. 16) both trails are labeled Upper Triangle Trail. SHT follows left branch for 0.4 miles.

(3.6) (3.0) Gill Creek Trail
SHT comes to intersection at large signpost and turns left (east) on Gill Creek Trail. Trail comes to views of St. Louis River Valley, then continues on narrow trail gradually descending to valley floor. After crossing scenic Gill Creek, trail climbs out of creek valley with nice views.

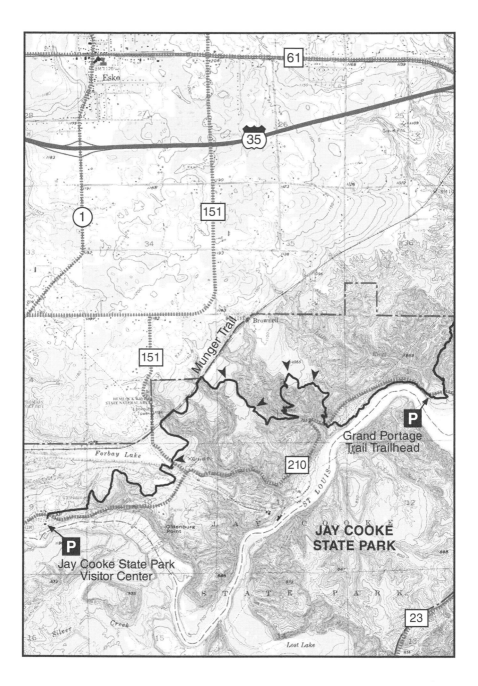

(4.7) (1.9) Oak Trail
At intersection of Gill Creek and Oak Trail (No. 21), SHT turns right (south) onto Oak Trail. Look for large oaks through here.

(5.0) (1.6) Intersection of Oak Trail and Grand Portage Trail
At this intersection (No. 22) both trails are labeled Grand Portage Trail. SHT follows branch to right. Trail descends steeply toward St. Louis River, crosses Hwy. 210, and continues on Grand Portage Trail along scenic St. Louis River for 0.8 miles before coming to Hwy. 210 once more. Trail follows Hwy. 210 for a short distance and then turns right on driveway into Grand Portage Trail trailhead parking lot.

(6.6) (0.0) Grand Portage Trail trailhead parking lot

Jay Cooke State Park Grand Portage Trailhead to Fond du Lac

4.2 miles

Section description: From the Grand Portage Trail parking lot at Jay Cooke State Park to Fond du Lac at 131st Ave. W.

Access and parking: *Directions to Beginning Trailhead:* State Park sticker needed to park in lot. 1) From I-35, take Carlton Exit #235 and go east on Hwy. 210 5.5 miles to Jay Cooke State Park Visitor Center and then continue another 3.9 miles to Grand Portage Trail trailhead parking lot on right. 2) From Hwy. 23–Hwy. 210 intersection, turn onto Hwy. 210 and go 2.4 miles to Grand Portage Trail parking lot on left. No overnight parking.

Facilities at beginning trailhead: none

Designated campsites on this section: Campground and four fee backpack sites at Jay Cooke State Park

Synopsis: This section begins with over a mile of hiking in Jay Cooke State Park. The trail then continues through hardwood forests with occasional pockets of large white pine trees. There are some steep climbs onto ridges and steep descents into river valleys. A highlight is the historic stone bridge over Mission Creek.

Mile-by-Mile Description

0.0 (4.2) Grand Portage Trail
SHT leaves parking lot following Grand Portage Trail for 0.2 miles. 300 feet after crossing Hwy. 210, SHT turns right, leaving Grand Portage Trail, and goes along ridge with large pine trees. Trail crosses power line and follows old road in predominantly maple forest.

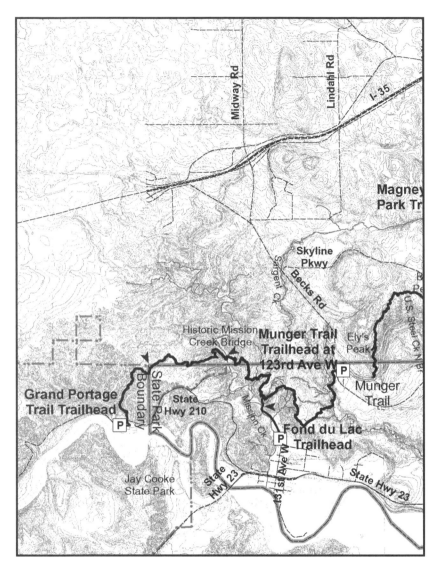

1.1 (3.1) State Park boundary sign

After crossing state park boundary marked by sign, SHT continues over high ridge. Trail descends ridge and continues through forest crossing branch of Mission Creek. Trail continues through woods passing an overlook before descending steeply to Mission Creek and historic bridge.

2.4 (1.8) Historic bridge on Mission Creek

SHT turns left on old Mission Creek Parkway, crosses historic bridge and after 150 feet, turns right into woods and crosses Mission Creek Parkway again before climbing steep hill and following high ridge. After descending ridge, SHT crosses two more branches of Mission Creek, then climbs to long bluff with nice pines. Trail descends to Duluth's Mission Creek Trail.

3.6 (0.6) Mission Creek Trail

Main SHT crosses Mission Creek Trail, bears left, and crosses bridge over tributary creek. Spur trail to parking lot turns downhill and follows Mission Creek Trail 600 feet to intersection with old road called Mission Creek Parkway. Spur trail turns left and follows road 0.5 miles to trailhead parking lot.

4.2 (0.0) Fond du Lac trailhead parking lot

Jay Cooke State Park

Jay Cooke State Park was established in 1915 when the St. Louis River Power Company donated 2,350 acres of land. In 1945, the state purchased additional land and added other sections over the years giving Jay Cooke State Park its present size of 8,818 acres. The rugged land formations of Jay Cooke State Park with the St. Louis River flowing through it enhance the beauty of the hardwood forests. Facilities include a visitor center built by the Civilian Conservation Corps in a stone Rustic Style in 1940, the Swinging Bridge over the St. Louis River, an 80-site campground, and 4 backpack campsites.

Fond du Lac to 123rd Avenue West

2.7 miles

Section description: From Fond du Lac at 131st Ave. W. to Munger Trail at 123rd Ave. W.

Access and parking: *Directions to Beginning Trailhead:* 1) From the south: From I-35, take Midway Rd. Exit #246. Go south 4.5 miles on Midway Rd./Beck's Rd. to Grand Ave./Commonwealth Ave./Hwy. 23. Turn right (south) and follow Hwy. 23 3.8 miles to 131st Ave. W. on right. Turn right on 131st Ave. W. and go 0.4 miles passing gate into trailhead parking lot in grassy area on left. 2) From the north: Take Hwy. 23/Grand Ave. Exit #251B and drive 8.7 miles to Fond du Lac. Turn right on 131st Ave. W. and go 0.4 miles passing gate into trailhead parking lot in grassy area on left. No overnight parking.

Facilities at beginning trailhead: none

Designated campsites on this section: none

Synopsis: In this section, the SHT climbs out of the Mission Creek Valley, continues on a high bluff with occasional views of St. Louis Bay and descends into picturesque Sargent Creek valley. A highlight is several pockets of old growth white pine trees.

Mile-by-Mile Description

0.0 (2.7) Fond du Lac at 131st Ave. W. trailhead
From parking lot, SHT spur trail follows old Mission Creek Parkway for 0.5 miles.

0.5 (2.2) Mission Creek Trail
SHT spur trail turns right onto Duluth's Mission Creek Trail at wooden sign. After 600 feet, spur trail meets SHT main trail. Main

SHT turns right, crosses bridge and ascends steep hill. SHT travels along pine ridge and then through maple-oak forest, through white pine grove, and then maple-aspen-birch forest. Trail comes to another towering white pine grove and then follows bluff before descending steeply on Andy's Switchback to Sargent Creek. SHT continues along Sargent Creek and then crosses creek on 50-foot bridge.

1.5 (1.2) Sargent Creek Bridge

After Sargent Creek Bridge, SHT follows creek, climbs steep hill, crosses Beck's Rd., and passes through aspen forest

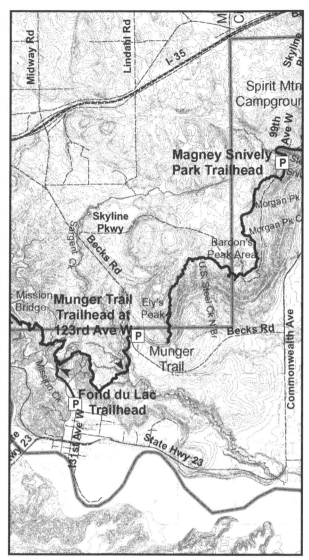

to trailhead sign. Main SHT continues across powerline to Munger Trail. 150-foot spur trail goes right to trailhead parking lot.

2.7 (0.0) Munger Trail trailhead parking lot

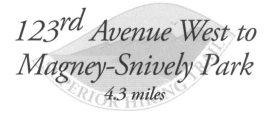

123rd Avenue West to Magney-Snively Park

4.3 miles

Section description: From Munger Trail at 123rd Ave. W. to Magney-Snively Park parking lot on Skyline Parkway

Access and parking: *Directions to Beginning Trailhead:* 1) From I-35, take Midway Rd. Exit #246. Go south on Midway Rd./Beck's Rd. 2.7 miles. Turn left on 123rd Ave. W. and go one block to parking lot on left. 2) On Grand Ave. in Duluth, go south to Beck's Rd. Turn right on Beck's Rd., go 1.8 miles to 123rd Ave. W., go right one block to parking lot. No overnight parking.

Facilities at beginning trailhead: none

Designated campsites on this section: none

Synopsis: This section begins on the paved Munger Trail. After 0.4 miles the SHT leaves the Munger Trail climbing to Ely's Peak with magnificent views. The trail then heads to Bardon's Peak with more views and through the Magney-Snively old growth forest.

Mile-by-Mile Description

0.0 (4.3) Munger Trail
SHT leaves parking lot on 150-foot spur trail to trailhead sign. Main SHT turns right, crosses powerline, turns right again onto paved Munger Trail and follows it for 0.4 miles to just before rock cut. SHT turns left at SHT signs and climbs rocky ridge to Ely's Peak with great views.

0.9 (3.4) Ely's Peak
SHT reaches ridge top just past Ely's Peak. 300-foot spur trail goes left (west) to summit of Ely's Peak at 1,219 feet. Main trail continues right

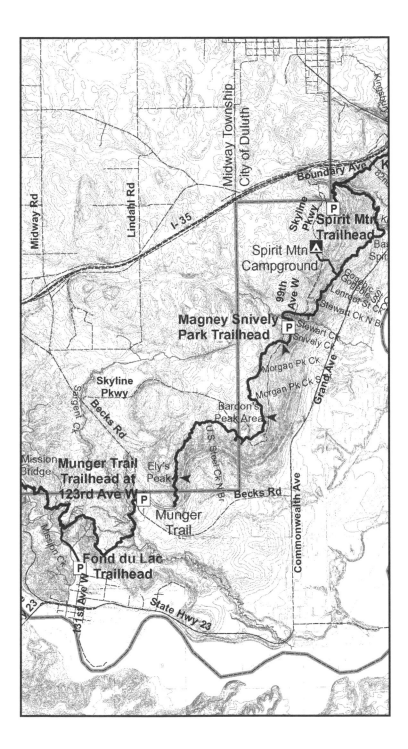

Skyline Parkway

The Superior Hiking Trail in Duluth winds back and forth across the historic and scenic Skyline Parkway. First conceived by William K. Rogers in 1888 and finished by Mayor Samuel Snively in the 1920s, this 25-mile-long roadway traverses the hillside high above St. Louis Bay and Lake Superior. Stagecoach rides and parties were frequent in the 1890s, while today the roadway is a State Scenic Byway. Skyline Parkway connects over twenty city parks.

(north) on rocky outcrops through mixed forest and overlooking fault-line valley. SHT enters maple-oak forest, crosses U.S. Steel Creek, passes two scenic overlooks, and then climbs gradually to Skyline Parkway.

2.4 (1.9) Bardon's Peak area
SHT crosses Skyline Parkway and travels through forest in Bardon's Peak area, passing numerous over-looks. SHT enters Magney-Snively old growth forest crossing Magney-Snively ski trail twice.

4.0 (0.3) Second crossing of Skyline Parkway
SHT crosses Skyline Parkway for second time and travels through pine grove coming to nice over-look. Trail continues through forest, crosses Snively Creek, and then comes to 350-foot spur trail to Magney-Snively Park parking lot.

4.3 (0.0) Magney-Snively Park trailhead parking lot

Magney-Snively Park to Spirit Mountain
3.2 miles

Section description: From the Magney-Snively Park parking lot on Skyline Parkway to Spirit Mountain Recreation Area on Skyline Parkway

Access and parking: *Directions to beginning trailhead:* From I-35, take Boundary Ave. Exit #249. Go south on Boundary Ave. past gas station, McDonald's, to T-stop. Turn left on Skyline Parkway (follow Spirit Mountain signs). Pass turnoff to Spirit Mountain chalet and continue another 1.5 miles on Skyline Parkway to parking lot on left. No overnight parking.

Facilities at beginning trailhead: none

Designated campsites on this section: Camping available from SHT spur trail to Spirit Mountain Campground

Synopsis: This section begins in Magney-Snively Park with beautiful Snively and Stewart creeks. The trail then goes through the Spirit Mountain Recreation Area with almost a mile along cascading Knowlton Creek.

Mile-by-Mile Description

0.0 (3.2) Magney-Snively Park parking lot
SHT spur trail leaves parking lot by trailhead sign and travels 350 feet to reach SHT main trail. SHT turns left and continues below Skyline Parkway for 0.2 miles until it reaches Skyline Parkway. Trail continues on Skyline Parkway for 0.2 mile road walk crossing Stewart Creek on stone bridge. 325 feet past 99th Ave. W., SHT turns right off road and enters maple-oak-pine forest. After Stewart Knob overlook, SHT

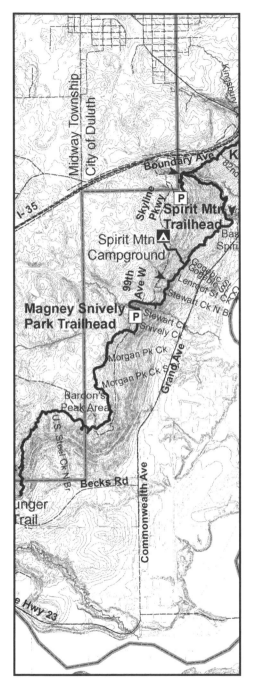

continues through forest, crosses old road and passes historic stone-walled section of north branch of Stewart Creek and old house foundation.

0.9 (2.3) Spirit Mountain Recreation Area

SHT crosses power line and enters Spirit Mountain Recreation Area. SHT gradually descends through forest crossing Lenroot St. Creek and the south and north branches of Gogebic St. Creek. Between the two creek branches is a 0.5 mile spur trail to Spirit Mountain Campground. Close to base of Spirit Mountain ski hill, SHT reaches old DWP railroad bed, follows DWP toward ski hill for 150 feet, and then turns right and descends through forest to base of ski hill.

1.9 (1.3) Base of ski hill/ Knowlton Creek

SHT comes into opening at base of ski hill. Trail continues between parking lot and ski hill through woods for 350 feet to Knowlton Creek. SHT turns left and climbs upstream along

Knowlton Creek. Trail climbs to DWP, turns right to follow DWP for 225 feet, turns left onto trail on ridge, turns left to follow Spirit Mountain maintenance road for 200 feet, then turns right to ascend along Knowlton Creek once again. Watch carefully for signs and blazing in this area. SHT continues uphill along Knowlton Creek for another 0.5 miles, then climbs away from creek, makes sharp right turn onto old roadbed and continues to Knowlton Creek Bridge.

2.9 (0.3) Knowlton Creek Bridge
At Knowlton Creek Bridge, a 0.3 mile spur trail does not cross bridge but heads uphill, turns left, travels through maple forest and crosses large parking lot to reach trailhead parking lot by Duluth Alpine Club building. Main SHT crosses bridge.

3.2 (0.0) Spirit Mountain trailhead parking lot

Spirit Mountain Recreation Area

The 175-acre Spirit Mountain Recreation Area was created in 1973. The dramatic hillside location features beautiful hardwood forests, cascading Knowlton Creek, downhill and cross-country skiing and snowshoeing in winter, a 73-site campground, five walk-in campsites, and three miles of the Superior Hiking Trail through the area. A 0.5 mile spur trail goes from the SHT main trail to the campground.

Spirit Mountain to Kingsbury Creek
2.0 miles

Section description: From Spirit Mountain Recreation Area on Skyline Parkway to Kingsbury Creek behind the Lake Superior Zoo at the end of Waseca St.

Access and parking: *Directions to beginning trailhead:* From I-35, take Boundary Ave. Exit #249. Go south on Boundary Ave. past gas station, McDonald's, to T-stop. Turn left on Skyline Parkway (follow Spirit Mountain signs). Take left turn to Spirit Mountain Chalet, go 2 blocks to trailhead parking lot on left by Duluth Alpine Club building. No overnight parking.

Facilities at beginning trailhead: none

Designated campsites on this section: none

Synopsis: In this section, the SHT descends to Knowlton Creek and then climbs steeply to go through forests alternating with open meadows with rock outcrops and nice views. The section ends with a spur trail that descends along cascading Kingsbury Creek.

Mile-by-Mile Description

0.0 (2.0) Spirit Mountain parking lot (by Duluth Alpine Club building)
SHT spur trail (shared with bikes) starts by trailhead sign, follows edge of large parking lot and enters woods near back of parking lot. Spur trail descends 0.3 miles to Knowlton Creek Bridge to reach main SHT. Main SHT crosses bridge, turns right, and follows old road downhill for 0.1 miles. Trail turns left and ascends steep hill on 138 steps. After passing through nice maple grove, SHT continues through forest mixed with open meadows, rock outcrops and glimpses of St. Louis Bay.

1.4 (0.6) Duluh's Kingsbury Creek Trail

SHT comes to Kingsbury Creek and turns right following Duluth's Kingsbury Creek Trail 0.2 miles downstream. Trail reaches old road and turns left and crosses Kingsbury Creek on bridge. Main trail continues straight across old road and enters woods again. 0.4-mile spur trail to trailhead parking lot turns right, continues downhill on Kingsbury Creek Trail and then on old road, goes through old parking lot and then follows fence behind zoo to trailhead parking lot at end of Waseca Street.

2.0 (0.0) Kingsbury Creek trailhead parking lot

Kingsbury Creek to Skyline Parkway at Getchell/Highland

3.2 miles

Section description: From Kingsbury Creek behind the Lake Superior Zoo at the end of Waseca St. to Skyline Parkway at the intersection of Getchell Rd. and Highland St.

Access and parking: *Directions to beginning trailhead:* 1) From the south: take I-35 Cody St. Exit #251A and continue on Cody St. for 0.3 miles. Turn right on N. 63rd Ave. W. and go 0.6 miles. Turn right on Grand Ave. and 0.7 miles. Turn right on Waseca St. (between 69th Ave. W. and 72nd Ave. W.) and go 0.2 miles to Dead End sign at trailhead parking lot. 2) From the north: take I-35 Grand Ave./Hwy. 23 Exit #251B and go right 0.8 miles on Grand Ave. to Waseca St. Turn right on Waseca St. and go 0.2 miles to Dead End sign at trailhead parking lot. No overnight parking.

Facilities at beginning trailhead: none

Designated campsites on this section: none

Synopsis: This section begins with a spur trail that climbs along the Kingsbury Creek. The SHT then meanders through the woods crossing several small creeks. The section ends with over a half a mile climb along scenic Keene Creek.

Mile-by-Mile Description

0.0 (3.2) Kingsbury Creek trailhead parking lot
A 0.4-mile spur trail leaves parking lot, goes behind zoo, and heads uphill following old road and then Duluth's Kingsbury Creek Trail. At intersection with main SHT by bridge, SHT turns right and goes through mixed forest with rocky outcrops.

1.1 (2.1) 68th Ave. W. Creek

SHT crosses snowmobile bridge with metal guard rails at 68th Ave. W. Creek and then enters aspen-birch forest alternating with open fields. Trail crosses 62nd Ave. W. Creek and then the West Branch of Keene Creek.

1.6 (1.6) West Branch of Keene Creek

After crossing creek SHT goes under elevated I-35 on old road, turns left and climbs hillside and travels through woods to Cody Street. Trail crosses Cody St. and follows N. 66th Ave. W. for one block, then turns left and follows Westgate Blvd. for two blocks. SHT turns right uphill following snowmobile trail for 200 feet, turns right again, crosses powerline and heads into alder woods.

2.5 (0.7) Keene Creek

SHT reaches main branch of Keene Creek and follows creek

upstream. Trail climbs steeply to cross Highland St. and Skyline Parkway over guard railing and continues to parking lot.

3.2 (0.0) Skyline Parkway trailhead parking lot

Skyline Parkway at Highland/ Getchell to Skyline Parkway at North 24th Avenue West

5.7 miles

Section description: From Skyline Parkway at the intersection of Highland St. and Getchell Rd. to the intersection of Skyline Parkway and North 24th Ave. W.

Access and parking: *Directions to beginning trailhead:* 1) From the south, take I-35 Boundary Ave. Exit #249. Turn left, cross bridge, then take right onto Skyline Parkway. Drive 2.4 miles to trailhead at intersection of Skyline Parkway, Getchell Rd. and Highland St. 2) From the north, take I-35 Central Ave. Exit #252. Turn right and go 0.8 miles uphill on Central Ave. Turn left on Highland St. and go 1.1 miles to intersection of Skyline Parkway. Cross Skyline Parkway to trailhead parking lot on right. Overnight parking okay.

Facilities at beginning trailhead: none

Designated campsites on this section: none

Synopsis: In this dramatic section, the SHT continues climbing along Keene Creek. The trail then winds through a beautiful mature maple-oak forest with little creeks crossing the trail. Much of the rest of the section is on the ridgeline with great views before descending to Miller Creek.

Mile-by-Mile Description

0.0 (5.7) Skyline Parkway parking lot

SHT leaves parking lot on east end (right end when facing trailhead sign), crosses Skyline Parkway and comes to old historic bridge over Keene Creek. Trail crosses bridge, turns left, and continues upstream past old stone pump house and scenic waterfalls. Trail crosses Skyline Parkway again and enters forest.

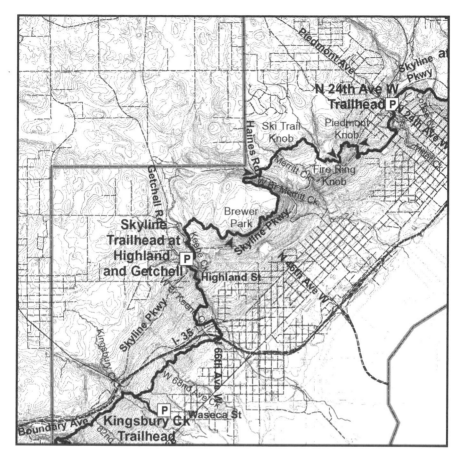

1.0 (4.7) Brewer Park

SHT enters Brewer Park and travels through maple-oak forest. Trail continues along Brewer Ridge for 1.4 miles with great views. Trail descends from ridge, turns right following snowmobile trail and reaches the west branch of Merritt Creek.

2.8 (2.9) West Branch of Merritt Creek

After crossing the West Branch of Merritt Creek on a culvert, SHT crosses Haines Rd. and enters predominantly maple forest crossing Piedmont Ski Trails twice and then climbs to Ski Trail Knob with great views. Trail crosses Merritt Creek and climbs to Fire Ring Knob.

Duluth's City Parks

Duluth, with a population of 86,000, has over 11,000 acres in its city park system, including over 125 parks, playgrounds and public places. There are over 53 miles of hiking trails in the city, not counting the Superior Hiking Trail. The SHT crosses many of these parks as it winds its way through Duluth. Many of the parks, such as Chester Creek Park and Lincoln Park, feature cascading creeks with waterfalls. Enger Park features gorgeous flower beds, a replica of an ancient Japanese bell, and the famous stone Enger Tower.

3.9 (1.8) Fire Ring Knob

After descent from knob SHT climbs to Grassy Knob and then continues to Piedmont Knob 1,300 feet in elevation with Lake Superior below at 602 feet. Trail descends and crosses Skyline Parkway.

4.6 (1.1) Skyline Parkway

After crossing Skyline Parkway, SHT descends through alder thicket passing Aspen Knob and continuing through alders. Trail comes to clearing and turns left following old road by enclosed city water reservoir. SHT crosses N. 27th Ave. W. and continues straight on W. 10th St. for one block until just past the street sign for Lincoln Parkway. SHT turns sharply left into woods. Trail crosses branch of Miller Creek, crosses N. 25th Ave. W., crosses Lincoln Park Drive, and then crosses bridge over Miller Creek. After bridge, SHT turns left and follows Duluth's Miller Creek Trail upstream to N. 24th Ave. W. and crosses street to parking lot.

5.7 (0.0) Parking lot at intersection of N. 24th Ave. W. and Skyline Parkway

Skyline Parkway at North 24th Avenue West to Enger Park

1.7 miles

Section description: From the intersection of Skyline Parkway and N. 24th Ave. W. to the Twin Ponds parking lot at Enger Park

Access and parking: *Directions to beginning trailhead:* From I-35, take Piedmont Ave./Hwy. 53 Exit #255A uphill 1.5 miles, turn left at stoplight onto Piedmont Ave., take first left onto N. 24th Ave. W., cross Skyline Parkway, and take left into parking lot. Overnight parking okay.

Facilities at beginning trailhead: none

Designated campsites on this section: none

Synopsis: In this section, after heading through an old city park, the SHT goes below Enger golf course and through city tree plantations and Enger Park. On the pine-studded trail through Enger Park, there is a spur trail to the stone Enger Tower, which provides stunning views of the surrounding area. The trail through Enger Park has lovely gardens, a historic bell, and nice views on the descent to Twin Ponds, a local swimming area.

Mile-by-Mile Description

0.0 (1.7) N. 24th Ave. W. trailhead parking lot
SHT leaves parking lot uphill and to right and follows Skyline Parkway on sidewalk crossing Piedmont Ave. on bridge. Trail continues along Parkway for 200 feet past bridge and then bears right through wooded field. Trail continues through field and then enters woods coming to the "Forgotten Park." SHT descends hill and crosses Coffee Creek. Trail continues through pine trees, crosses Skyline Parkway, goes through woods, and crosses Hank Jensen Drive.

St. Louis
Bay

1.1 (0.6) Hank Jensen Drive

After Hank Jensen Drive, SHT follows left side of Enger Tower Rd. for 80 feet. Trail goes along edge of flower bed and then turns sharply left behind flower bed and follows Duluth's Enger Park Trail. Spur trail on right to Enger Tower. After spur trail, SHT continues through pine woods, passes historic bell, and follows "Scenic View" trail down to Skyline Parkway. Trail crosses Skyline Parkway. Main SHT goes to right after Skyline Parkway. Spur trail to parking lot goes down stairs, passes swimming area, and follows grassy lawn with benches around pond, climbs bank, and crosses Skyline Parkway to the Twin Ponds parking lot.

1.7 (0.0) Twin Ponds trailhead parking lot

Enger Park to The Rose Garden
3.8 miles

Section description: From the Twin Ponds parking lot at Enger Park to the Rose Garden on the Duluth Lakewalk

Access and parking: *Directions to beginning trailhead:* From I-35, take Piedmont Ave./Hwy. 53 Exit #255A uphill 1.5 miles, turn left at stoplight onto Piedmont Ave., take first left onto N. 24th Ave. W., turn left onto Skyline Parkway and go 1.5 miles to Twin Ponds trailhead parking lot. No overnight parking.

Facilities at beginning trailhead: none

Designated campsites on this section: none

Synopsis: At the beginning of this section, the SHT descends over half a mile down the hill through undeveloped Central Park and Point of Rocks Park. The trail then begins its more urban route through the city of Duluth following paved trails and sidewalks by Bayfront Park, Canal Park and the Duluth Lakewalk with beautiful views of Lake Superior.

Mile-by-Mile Description

0.0 (3.8) Twin Ponds parking lot
From parking lot, a 440-foot SHT spur trail crosses Skyline Parkway to bank of pond, descends bank and goes around pond to concrete staircase and up stairs to reach main trail. Main SHT turns left and enters birch woods by yellow metal post through small boulders. Trail meanders through woods, crosses W. 5th St., and enters Duluth's undeveloped Central Park. Trail continues downhill through woods dotted with rock outcrops and nice stand of jack pine.

Duluth Lakewalk

The Duluth Lakewalk is a 4.2-mile multipurpose non-motorized walkway that extends along the Lake Superior shoreline from Bayfront Park to 27th Avenue East. It's a great opportunity to stroll along Lake Superior or to play on the rocky shore. Watercraft of all kinds, including giant iron ore freighters, pass through the shipping canal and under the Aerial Lift Bridge. The Lakewalk goes through Leif Erickson Park and the Rose Garden with 2,000 rose bushes of 99 varieties and numerous other trees, shrubs and flowers.

0.4 (3.4) W. 3rd Street

After street, SHT continues downhill through woods and turns left and then left again to follow along rock ledge above old quarry with views of harbor. Trail comes to N. 14th Ave. W., turns right and follows avenue downhill for 325 feet crossing W. 1st St. Trail enters woods again by three small boulders and goes though Duluth's Point of Rocks Park. Trail descends series of rock steps through woods, then descends from rocky ledge turning right onto old asphalt pad. Trail heads diagonally to right across asphalt pad, enters woods again, turns left, and follows rock ledge with good views of harbor.

0.8 (3.0) Intersection of Glen Place and W. Michigan Street

SHT crosses Glen Place, turns right, and crosses W. Michigan St. to bus stop bench. Trail turns left and travels 0.1 miles on sidewalk to I-35 overpass. Trail turns right, crosses I-35 on pedestrian overpass, turns left and descends long concrete ramp, and then travels on asphalt path under elevated I-35 to Railroad Street.

1.3 (2.5) Railroad Street

SHT crosses Railroad St., turns left and follows sidewalk 0.1 miles along Railroad St. Trail turns right on S. 5th Ave. W. At curve in street, SHT follows sidewalk and then turns left and follows ashpalt path to meet S. 5th Ave. W. again. Trail turns right on S. 5th Ave. W. and travels on gravel path to Harbor Dr.

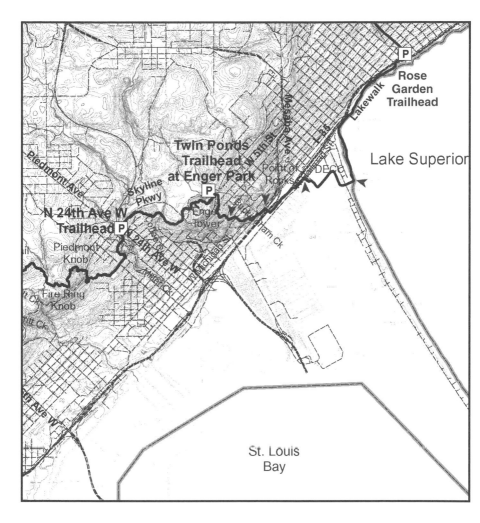

1.6 (2.2) Harbor Drive

SHT turns left on Harbor Dr. and follows sidewalk along harbor past Duluth Entertainment and Convention Center (DECC) and Vista Fleet office. Trail comes to blue bridge over harbor marina, crosses bridge, turns right following sidewalk by blue railing overlooking harbor to Ship Canal, and then follows concrete walkway under Aerial Lift Bridge and by Marine Museum. Trail turns left onto sidewalk, leaves Ship Canal and continues along Lake Superior. Watch for SHT logo stickers along this area.

2.2 (1.6) Duluth's Lakewalk

SHT continues on sidewalk on Duluth's scenic Lakewalk along Lake Superior for next 1.4 miles. Various stairs from Lakewalk lead to city restaurants and businesses. Trail enters Leif Erikson Park passing Viking ship and comes to concrete stairs and bridge leading up to Rose Garden. Trail ascends stairs, crosses bridge, follows sidewalk around Rose Garden and then continues to Rose Garden Parking Lot.

3.8 (0.0) Rose Garden parking lot at intersection of London Rd. and N. 14th Ave. East

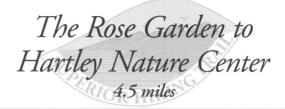

The Rose Garden to Hartley Nature Center
4.5 miles

Section description: From the Rose Garden at the Duluth Lakewalk to the Hartley Nature Center on Woodland Ave.

Access and parking: *Directions to beginning trailhead:* The Rose Garden parking lot is at intersection of London Rd. and N. 14th Ave. E. From I-35, take 21st Ave. E. Exit #258, turn left at stop sign and go 200 feet to London Road. Turn left on London Rd. at traffic light and go 7 blocks to parking lot on left. The Rose Garden parking lot is posted for 3-hour parking only. If planning a longer hike, there is plenty of free parking along London Road. Overnight parking okay on London Rd.

Facilities at beginning trailhead: Public bathroom

Designated campsites on this section: none

Synopsis: In this section, the SHT climbs the hill on sidewalks and then continues through Chester Creek Park along Chester Creek for almost a mile. After connecting with the Bagley Nature Center trails at the University of Minnesota Duluth, the trail meanders through the forests and ridges of Hartley Park before coming to the Hartley Nature Center.

Mile-by-Mile Description

0.0 (4.5) Rose Garden parking lot
From intersection of London Rd. and N. 14th Ave. E., SHT crosses London Rd. and follows sidewalk uphill on N. 14th Ave. E. on left side for 0.4 miles to E. 4th St. Watch for blue blazes on power poles.

0.4 (4.1) Chester Creek Trail
SHT crosses E. 4th St. to entrance of Duluth's Chester Creek Trail and follows scenic trail for 0.9 miles. At fork in trail 0.1 miles after trail entrance, SHT takes left fork over bridge and continues on left (west) side of creek to Skyline Parkway by rock wall.

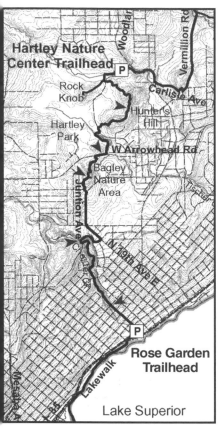

Hartley Nature Center Trailhead

Rock Knob

Hartley Park

Bagley Nature Area

Rose Garden Trailhead

Lake Superior

1.3 (3.2) Skyline Parkway

At Skyline Parkway, SHT turns right on sidewalk, crosses bridge and follows Skyline Parkway on right side 0.2 miles to W. Kent Road. Trail crosses Skyline Parkway and continues along W. Kent Rd. on sidewalk for 0.1 miles to N. 19th Ave. E. Trail crosses N. 19th Ave. E., turns left and continues on sidewalk on N. 19th Ave. E. for 0.2 miles to intersection of 19th Ave. E./College St./Junction Ave. on University of Minnesota Duluth (UMD) campus. Trail crosses College St. at stoplight, turns left traveling 50 feet to Junction Ave., then turns right following Junction Ave. for 0.4 miles past Parking Lot P, Niagara Court, Parking Lot Q and part of Parking Lot U on opposite side of street.

2.2 (2.3) UMD's Bagley Nature Trails

At crosswalk by Parking Lot U, SHT crosses Junction Ave. into Parking Lot U, goes to back of lot, and follows blacktop trail through woods 40 feet to dead end of E. Buffalo St., crosses street and goes into woods 100 feet to gravel road. Trail turns left onto road, goes 25 feet, and then turns left onto Bagley trail. SHT follows Bagley trail for 0.2 miles, turns right back to gravel road, and then turns left and follows road into open area on hilltop with overlook viewing platform with great views. SHT continues north past fire ring into woods.

SHT descends series of wooden steps and travels downhill zigzagging left and then right. SHT continues downhill crossing another Bagley trail and then crossing major bridge over small branch of Tischer Creek. After bridge, SHT turns right and travels through woods, turns left at fork in trail, goes 170 feet, then turns left again and continues 200 feet to Arrowhead Rd.

2.7 (1.8) Arrowhead Rd. and Hartley Park

SHT turns right on Arrowhead Rd. and follows road on right side on sidewalk for 0.1 miles to SHT post just before West Branch of Tischer Creek. Trail turns left crossing Arrowhead Rd. and continues north through woods. Trail rises to a T-intersection, turns right and travels through woods crossing a short local use trail to rocky knoll. Trail enters Hartley Park and continues through woods with large spruce, white pine, and cedar.

SHT turns right and crosses wide bridge on West Branch of Tischer Creek. Trail comes to old Hartley Rd., turns left, follows road for 200 feet, then turns right off road and through woods dotted with white pine. SHT crosses a Hartley trail and climbs uphill through hardwood forest.

Bagley Nature Area

The University of Minnesota Duluth's William R. Bagley Nature Area began with the donation of 16 acres from Dr. William Bagley for recreation, hawk watching, and plant study. Additional donations and purchases brought it to its present-day 59 acres. The mission of the Bagley Nature Area is to provide educational and recreational experiences emphasizing year round conservation, environmental education, and outdoor recreation. The overlook viewing platform on Rock Hill has magnificent views.

3.8 (0.7) Hunter's Hill ridge top

SHT comes to top of ridge with nice views at an elevation of 1,365 feet. Trail gradually descends from ridge, crosses a Hartley trail, and meanders through woods eventually coming to older pine plantation. Trail turns left and crosses two Hartley trails before coming to wide trail intersection by pet clean-up station. After going 50 feet toward pond, a spur trail to left goes 0.3 miles to Rock Knob overlook with great views. Main trail turns right and goes over dam on Hartley Pond. After dam, SHT turns right, travels through field, and comes to Hartley Nature Center.

4.5 (0.0) Hartley Nature Center and parking lot

Hartley Nature Center
to Martin Road
3.1 miles

Section description: From Hartley Nature Center on Woodland Ave. to the Martin Rd. parking lot.

Access and parking: *Directions to beginning trailhead:* From I-35, take 21st Ave. East Exit #258. Turn left on 21st Ave. E. and go 0.7 miles up hill. Turn right on Woodland Ave. and go 2.6 miles. Turn left on Hartley Nature Center driveway and go to parking lot. No overnight parking.

Directions to Martin Rd. trailhead: From I-35, take 21st Ave. East Exit #258. Turn left on 21st Ave. E. and go 0.7 miles up hill. Turn right on Woodland Ave. and go 1.2 miles. Turn right on Snively Rd. and go 1.0 miles to intersection with Jean Duluth Rd. Continue straight on Jean Duluth Rd. and go 1.9 miles. Turn left on Martin Rd. and go 1.2 miles to trailhead parking lot on left. Overnight parking okay.

Directions to end of spur at Hawk Ridge: Take I-35 to its end at 26th Ave. E. and London Road. Continue straight on London Rd. for 1.8 miles. Turn left on 45th Ave. E. and go 1.2 miles. Turn left on Glenwood St. and go 0.7 miles. Turn sharply right on Skyline Parkway and go 0.6 miles to trailhead sign on left. Watch closely for sign and park along road.

Facilities at beginning trailhead: Nature Center with bathrooms, displays, and a sitting area

Designated campsites on this section: none

Synopsis: After traveling along scenic Tischer Creek, the SHT travels on almost a mile of sidewalk and road before entering the woods again and continuing through Downer Park to Martin Road. This section also has an option to take the 1.7-mile spur trail to Hawk Ridge Nature Reserve.

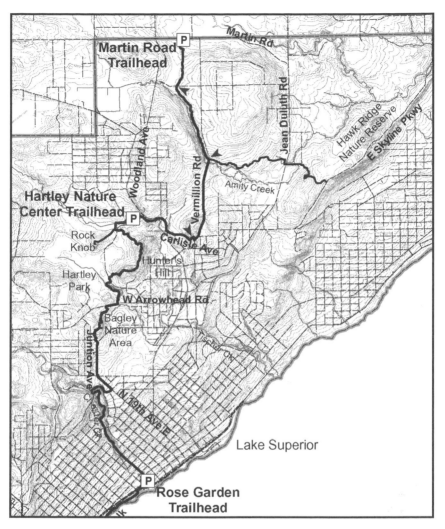

Mile-by-Mile Description

0.0 (3.1) Hartley Nature Center

SHT leaves parking lot at east end toward Woodland Ave. Trail turns right out of parking lot and travels by Tischer Creek for 0.2 miles to trail fork. Trail follows fork to left uphill to huge cottonwood tree and crosses grassy lawn to bus stop bench on Woodland Ave. Trail turns right (southeast) and follows Woodland Ave. on sidewalk on right side 0.2 miles to Fairmont St. Trail turns left crossing Woodland Ave. to

Hartley Nature Center

The Hartley Nature Center, an independent non-profit organization, is located within Duluth's 660-acre Hartley Park. The beautiful building uses solar panels and geothermal heat from a ground-source heat pump to heat the building. Programs for the general public and area schools include natural history topics ranging from bird banding to beaver ecology to solar energy technology. Highlights include several miles of trails, Hartley Pond, and Tischer Creek. Snowshoes and cross-country skis are available for rent in the winter.

Carlisle Ave. SHT follows Carlisle Ave. east 0.3 miles to Grove Street, turns left and follows Grove St. 250 feet to Vermilion St, then turns right and follows Vermilion. St. 185 feet to Vermilion Road.

0.8 (2.3) Vermilion Rd.
At intersection of Vermilion St. and Vermilion Rd., SHT turns sharply left and travels on Vermilion Rd. for 0.9 miles passing between Forest Hill and Park Hill cemeteries.

1.7 (1.4) Amity Creek/spur trail to Hawk Ridge
From left (west) side of Vermilion Rd., as road starts to rise over culvert for Amity Creek, main SHT turns left into woods entering Duluth's Downer Park. Watch carefully for trail entrance. On right (east) side of Vermilion Rd., there is a 1.7-mile spur trail to Hawk Ridge.

Optional spur trail to Hawk Ridge, 1.7 miles
After crossing Vermilion Rd. and entering woods, spur trail follows Amity Creek on rise above creek coming to pond with beaver-felled trees. Trail leaves creek continuing through woods, crosses snowmobile trail, and comes to Jean Duluth Rd. Trail turns right and travels along road in ditch for 260 feet, turns left and crosses Jean Duluth Rd., and travels on Amity St. for 0.2 miles. Trail leaves Amity St. on right and continues through woods with interesting rock outcrops to Skyline Parkway.

Main SHT continues through Downer Park, following slope above Amity Creek through maple-oak-birch forest. Note rhyolite rock strewn throughout this area. Trail leaves creek, crosses snowmobile trail twice, and continues through woods.

2.6 (0.5) Pleasant View Rd.
SHT crosses Pleasant View Rd. and travels through predominantly aspen forest. Trail comes to series of long boardwalks through ash wetlands, then crosses a small branch of Amity Creek before coming to parking lot on Martin Rd.

3.1 (0.0) Martin Rd. trailhead parking lot

Hawk Ridge

The 315-acre Hawk Ridge Nature Reserve provides some of North America's best autumn hawk watching. A seasonal average of over 94,000 raptors migrate past Hawk Ridge from mid-August through November each year. Bird-banding, bird counting, and public programs are provided by the Hawk Ridge Bird Observatory, an independent non-profit organization. There is also an extensive hiking trail network at the Reserve.

Trail Construction between Martin Road and Fox Farm Road/East Trailhead

The Superior Hiking Trail currently ends at the Martin Road trailhead in Duluth. It begins again at the Fox Farm Road/East Trailhead, a gap of about 20 miles. Plans call for the Superior Hiking Trail Association to continue to build the SHT through this area from 2010 to 2013. Scouting for the route has begun, but no easements or permits have been obtained.

The North Shore State Trail (NSST), which is a state trail built for snowmobiling but that allows horseback riding, mountain biking, and hiking, begins at the Martin Road trailhead and crosses Fox Farm Road 0.1 miles north of the Fox Farm Road/East Trailhead parking lot, so hikers could use the NSST as a connector trail. It should be noted, however, that some of the trail is very wet (since it goes on frozen wetlands in the winter) and the grass is not mowed in summer, making it shoulder-high in some areas. The NSST is mowed in early fall to make it easier to groom the trail in winter so hiking conditions improve considerably in the fall.

The NSST can be hiked in two segments. The first segment from the Martin Road parking lot to the Normanna Road parking lot is 12.5 miles. The second segment from the Normanna Road parking lot to the SHT Fox Farm/East Trailhead is 11.1 miles.

Trail construction progress updates are on the SHTA website at www.shta.org. The website also has information on how to volunteer for trail construction projects.

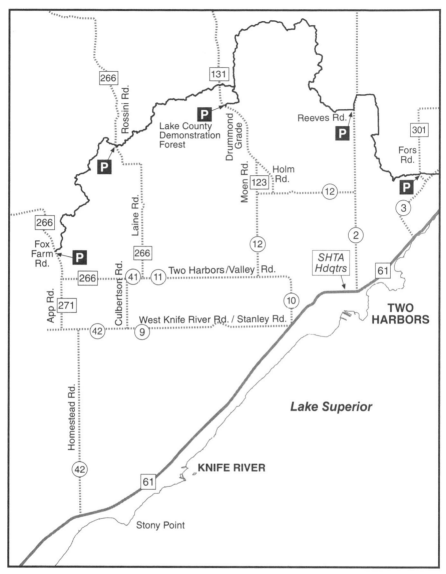

Trailhead Parking Lot Locator Map for trail sections Fox Farm Road/ East Trailhead through Co. Rd. 301 (Fors Rd.)

Fox Farm Road East/Trailhead to Rossini Road

6.4 miles

Section description: Fox Farm Road/East Trailhead to Rossini Road

Access and parking: *Directions to beginning trailhead:* From Hwy. 61 milepost 14.9, turn north (inland) on Homestead Rd. (Co. Rd. 42) and go 5.75 miles. Turn left (west) on West Knife River Rd. and go 0.5 miles. Turn right (north) on App Rd. and go 1.5 miles to intersection with Two Harbors Rd on right. App Rd. changes to Fox Farm Rd. at this intersection. Continue straight (north) on Fox Farm Rd. 0.9 miles to trailhead parking lot on left. Overnight parking okay.

Facilities at beginning trailhead: none

Designated campsites on this section: one

Synopsis: This relatively level section features the lovely west branch of the Knife River, one of the major river systems in St. Louis County. One of the highlights is a series of old beaver ponds with 28-inch diameter beaver-chewed trees dotting the trail. The trail rises in a couple of places for views of the surrounding countryside and Lake Superior, 12 miles away.

Mile-by-Mile Description

0.0 (6.4) Fox Farm Rd. trailhead parking lot

From parking lot, SHT crosses Fox Farm Rd. and travels through small wetland on boardwalk. After crossing open field, trail comes to North Shore State Trail (snowmobile trail). Just before snowmobile trail bridge on West Branch of the Knife River, trail turns left (north) by brown kiosk and follows scenic river upstream. Trail leaves river and goes through ash forest in low area and then starts to climb to nice maple-basswood forest. Look for large old white pine stumps.

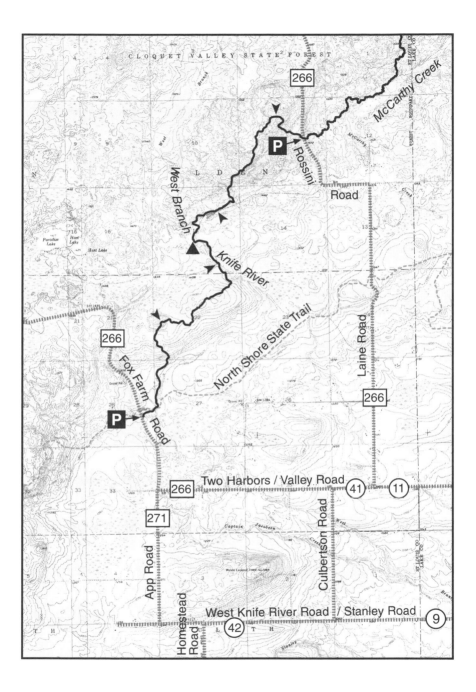

1.3 (5.1) Fox Farm Hill

SHT comes to young red pine plantation and continues through it for next 0.5 miles. Trail climbs to Fox Farm Hill with sweeping views on both sides of hill. After leaving pine plantation, SHT travels though alternating balsam and hardwood forests eventually coming again to West Branch of Knife River. Before river, SHT crosses a long, straight road that was an old railroad grade.

2.7 (3.7) West Branch of Knife River

SHT follows river, passing through mixed forest dotted with small groves of white pine and large spruce trees. After crossing small tributary creek on bridge, SHT crosses snowmobile trail near snowmobile trail bridge. Watch signing and do not cross river here -- SHT bridge crossing of West Branch of Knife River is 0.1 miles further upstream. After bridge crossing, trail continues upstream to campsite.

3.5 (2.9) Big Bend Campsite

▲ Big Bend Campsite

Tent pads: 4
Water: from river
Setting: On West Branch of Knife River
Next campsite: 6.2 miles

After campsite, SHT continues along series of meadows that are old dried-up beaver ponds.

4.0 (2.4) Series of beaver ponds

After continuing through mixed forest, SHT comes to long series of beaver ponds lasting for 0.6 miles. At mid-point of ponds, trail crosses small stream. After more ponds, SHT starts to climb steeply and enters long stretch of mature maple forest dotted with white pine.

5.9 (0.5) Twelve-mile view

SHT comes to break in forest where you can see Lake Superior 12 miles away. Trail starts descending gradually through more open woods to Rossini Rd. trailhead.

6.4 (0.0) Rossini Rd. trailhead parking lot

Rossini Road to Lake County Demonstration Forest

6.9 miles

Section description: Rossini Road to the Lake County Demonstration Forest on Drummond Grade (Co Rd. 131)

Access and parking: *Directions to beginning trailhead:* At Hwy. 61 milepost 14.9, turn north (inland) on Homestead Rd. (Co. Rd. 42) and go 5.75 miles. Turn right (east) on West Knife River Rd. and go 1.5 miles. Turn left (north) on Culbertson Rd. and go 1.5 miles. Turn right (east) on Two Harbors Rd. and go 0.5 miles. Turn left (north) on Laine Rd. and go 3.5 miles. Turn left on Rossini Rd. and go 1.3 miles to trailhead parking lot on left. Overnight parking okay.

Facilities at beginning trailhead: none

Designated campsites on this section: two

Synopsis: Highlights of this section include lovely older maple forests and some scenic tributaries of the Knife River. There is evidence of historic railroad and some mining if you look carefully. The section ends by sharing the trails of the Lake County Demonstration Forest.

Mile-by-Mile Description

0.0 (6.9) Rossini Rd. trailhead parking lot

SHT crosses Rossini Rd. and enters mixed woods of balsam fir-birch-aspen-maple-basswood. Trail crosses wet area on bridge and then crosses three small bridges on tributaries of McCarthy Creek in area that shows regrowth from logging. Between third and fourth small bridges look carefully as trail rises to see old railroad cut. Narrow gauge railroads were used throughout this area for historic logging. Trail goes by several vernal ponds that have water in spring. Trail enters hardwood forest dotted with occasional large white pines. The large number of leatherwood shrubs throughout this area is noteworthy.

2.0 (4.9) Bridge on McCarthy Creek tributary

This is the fourth of four bridges on small tributaries. Note the clear water of this tributary. Trail continues alternating between mature maple forest and fir-aspen-birch forests.

3.3 (3.6) McCarthy Creek bridge and campsite

▲ McCarthy Creek Campsite

Tent pads: 2
Water: From McCarthy Creek
Setting: On McCarthy Creek, unreliable during dry conditions
Previous campsite: 6.4 miles
Next campsite: 1.2 miles

After campsite, SHT crosses bridge below lovely grass-lined waterfall. After leaving creek, trail goes through white pine stand, crosses dirt track, and continues through mixed forest.

4.1 (2.8) Old Drummond Rd.

SHT crosses Old Drummond Rd. and comes to area where trail is strewn with frost-shattered rock—watch your step carefully here.

4.4 (2.5) Ferguson tributary of the Knife River

Trail descends to boulder-filled river branch, crosses it on bridge and ascends to Ferguson Campsite.

▲ Ferguson Campsite

Tent pads: 2
Water: From river 100 yards from campsite
Setting: In spruce trees on hill above tributary of Knife River
Previous campsite: 1.2 miles
Next campsite: 7.6 miles

After campsite, SHT soon comes to land that was managed by noted local forester Don Ferguson and is now part of Lake County

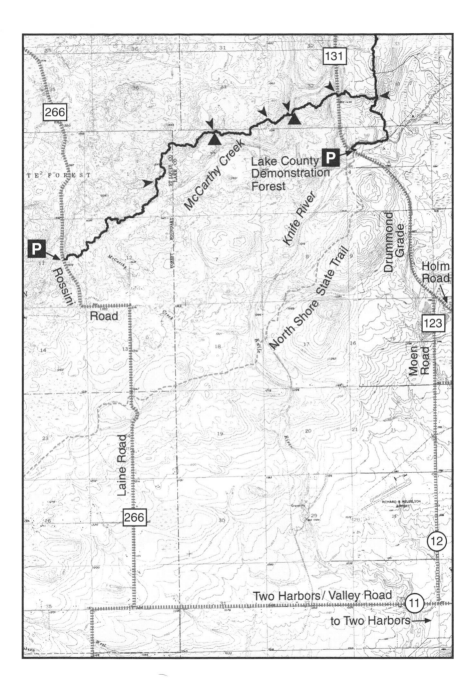

266

131

266

P

Lake County
Demonstration
Forest

McCarthy Creek

Knife River

P

Rossini

Road

North Shore State Trail

Drummond Grade

Holm
Road

123

Moen
Road

Laine Road

266

12

Two Harbors/ Valley Road

to Two Harbors

11

Demonstration Forest. This 400-acre site has a network of trails and is dedicated to historic interpretation, education, and forest management demonstrations.

5.1 (1.8) Drummond Grade

SHT comes to Drummond Grade, a gravel road that is a former railroad grade. At road, trail turns right (south) and goes on road for 100 feet and then turns left into woods on other side of road. Trail comes to "mystery hole," which is actually an old mining test pit. Trail comes to small logged area; watch carefully for trail blazing in this area. Trail continues through mixed forest with view of Lake Superior.

5.7 (1.2) Trail junction at SHT main trail and SHT spur trail

SHT comes to trail junction where SHT main trail turns left (north) and SHT spur trail turns right (south). After 0.5miles, SHT spur turns left (south) where it continues on Demonstration Forest trail called the Ferguson Trail/Orange Trail for 0.1 miles. SHT spur trail turns right (west) onto Gravel Pit Trail/Orange Trail by gate (make sure you don't turn onto North Shore State Trail – check for signs here) and travels on Gravel Pit Trail/Orange Trail 0.5 miles and then turns left (southeast) onto Knife River/Blue Trail and travels 333 feet to trailhead parking lot by kiosk and log outhouses.

6.9 (0.0) Lake County Demonstration Forest trailhead parking lot

Lake County Demonstration Forest to Reeves Road

11.0 miles

Section description: Lake County Demonstration Forest on Drummond Grade to Reeves Rd.

Access and parking: *Directions to beginning trailhead:* At Hwy. 61 milepost 26.0 in Two Harbors, turn north (inland) on Hwy. 2 (Lake Co. Rd. 2) and go 3.0 miles. Turn left on Hwy. 12 (Co. Rd. 12) and go 2.5 miles. Turn right on Holm Rd and go 0.5 miles. Turn left on Drummond Grade (Co. Rd. 131) and go 2.5 miles to parking lot on right. There is no defined parking lot here. Park along the side of the dirt road that goes in both directions when you turn in the driveway. Overnight parking okay.

Facilities at beginning trailhead: outhouses, picnic table, kiosk with brochures about the Lake County Demonstration Forest

Designated campsites on this section: one

Synopsis: The highlights of this section start with the Lake County Demonstration forest, which has an interesting collection of hiking trails, including an interpretive loop. The relatively level section also features several old growth maple forests and the scenic Stewart River.

Mile-by-Mile Description

0.0 (11.0) Lake County Demonstration Forest trailhead

SHT spur trail follows a series of Demonstration Forest trails for 1.2 miles to reach main SHT. Facing trailhead sign, SHT spur trail goes left (west) on Knife River/Blue Trail for 333 feet. SHT spur turns right (east) onto Gravel Pit/Orange Trail and goes for 0.5 miles coming to gates by Briton Pit Road. SHT spur turn left (north) on Ferguson/Orange Trail for 0.1 miles. At sign, SHT spur turns right off of Ferguson/Orange Trail to continue on SHT spur for another 0.5 miles to reach main SHT at intersection.

Donald D. Ferguson Lake County Demonstration Forest

The 400-acre Demonstration Forest was established in 2001 by Lake County due to the vision of Donald Ferguson, a long-time Lake County resident and forester. In the past, two historic railroad grades went through this area and a railroad camp was located at the site. Today the Demonstration Forest hosts a variety of hiking trails, including a unique 23-point interpretive loop of wetlands, wildlife openings, an old homestead, the Knife River, and various forest stands. The Superior Hiking Trail spur trail from this trailhead goes on a variety of the Demonstration Forest trails.

1.2 (9.8) SHT main trail
At intersection, main SHT turns right (north) to go on to Reeves Rd. trailhead (main SHT turns left to go to Rossini Rd. trailhead). SHT goes through mature maple forest and then young aspen forest.

1.9 (9.1) Mossy knobs
SHT climbs slightly to first one, than another nice rock outcrop covered in moss and reindeer lichen and continues in another nice maple forest.

2.6 (8.4) Red pine forest
Trail crosses old logging road and continues by large glacial erratic boulder and soon goes through long stretch of red pine forest. Trail skirts edge of large pond and continues through red pine forest.

4.0 (7.0) West Branch of Stewart River
SHT comes to the crystal clear West Branch of Stewart River and crosses river on small bridge.

4.5 (6.5) Old railroad cut
Trail comes to odd cut through two side hills. This was likely the grade for a historic narrow gauge railroad used for logging. After 0.2 miles, SHT enters area of trees cut by beavers. A short 109-foot spur leads to beaver pond. After going through mixed forest, SHT travels through young red pine stand and then descends gradually to Stewart River.

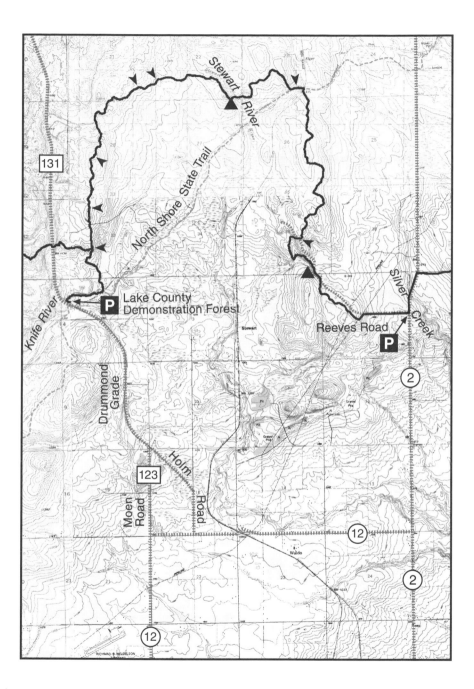

5.1 (5.9) Stewart River and Campsite

▲ Stewart River Campsite

Tent pads: 3
Water: From Stewart River
Setting: On Stewart River
Previous campsite: 7.6 miles
Next campsite: 4.3 miles

After crossing bridge at Stewart River, SHT crosses previously logged area replanted with young spruce. Trail goes back into mixed forest and then descends down side of rock ridge and crosses on small bridge to North Shore State Trail (NSST).

6.2 (4.8) North Shore State Trail

SHT turns left (east) and follows NSST for 0.2 miles going under railroad overpass (look for taconite pellets) and then comes to yellow gate. Trail turns right (south) at gate onto Dufresne Rd. SHT follows road for 175 feet, turns left (south) into mixed forest and then comes to mature maple forest. Look for an exceptionally large basswood tree in this area. SHT comes to old logging road and turns left following road for 0.1 miles, then veers right off road into another nice maple forest.

8.7 (2.3) First crossing of Reeves Rd.

SHT comes to first of three crossings of Reeves Rd. through young white pine plantation and then goes along stretch of interesting rock outcrops and then wooded cliff top. Right before second crossing of Reeves Rd. at 9.4 miles is lovely Reeves Falls. At road, SHT turns right onto road and goes for 194 feet and then turns left into woods again. Where main SHT turns left off road into woods, on right is spur trail to Reeves Falls Campsite.

▲ Reeves Falls Campsite

Tent pads: 3
Water: From stream below falls
Setting: In woods above small tributary of Stewart River
Previous campsite: 4.3 miles
Next campsite: 5.9 miles

At third crossing of Reeves Rd. at 9.6 miles, trail goes straight across road, then continues through woods and crosses pipeline opening and then powerline opening. SHT comes to Reeves Rd. again by yellow gate and turns right (east) and follows road 0.5 miles to trailhead parking lot on right.

11.0 (0.0) Reeves Rd. trailhead parking lot

Reeves Road to Lake County Road 301
5.4 miles

Section description: Reeves Rd. to Lake Co. Rd. 301 (Fors Rd.)

Access and parking: *Directions to beginning trailhead:* At Hwy. 61 milepost 26.0 in Two Harbors, turn north on Hwy. 2 (Lake Co. Rd. 2) and go 5.5 miles. Turn left on Reeves Rd. and take immediate left into trailhead parking lot. Overnight parking okay.

Facilities at beginning trailhead: none

Designated campsites on this section: one

Synopsis: Highlights of this section include a steep rock cliff face where the trail goes down the cliff on rock stairs and almost two miles of trail along cascading Silver Creek.

Mile-by-Mile Description

0.0 (5.4) Reeves Road trailhead parking lot
From parking lot, SHT turns north (uphill) and follows Hwy. 2 (Co. Rd. 2) on shoulder for 0.5 miles. Walk on left facing traffic. Just before Dixie's Bar and Grill, SHT turns right (east) onto snowmobile trail and follows it for 0.5 miles. Watch carefully for signs here. Stay on trail here and yield to snowmobiles in winter. SHT turns right (south) off of snowmobile trail into mixed forest and then through a nice maple forest. Trail continues through mixed forest to rock cliff.

1.3 (4.1) Rock cliff
After descending basalt rock cliff on rock stairs, SHT descends gradually through woods, crosses Gun Club Rd., and continues through mixed forest and some fern-laden openings to scenic Silver Creek.

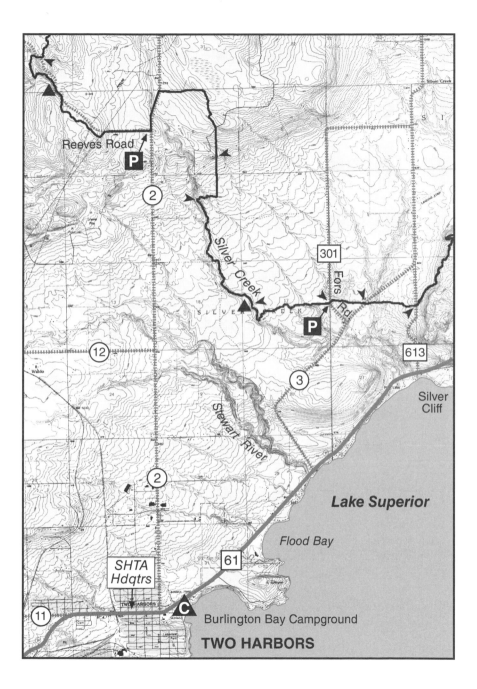

Reeves Road

P

(2)

Silver Creek

301

Fors Rd

P

12

Waldo

3

613

Silver Cliff

Stewart River

(2)

Lake Superior

Flood Bay

61

SHTA Hdqtrs

11

C

Burlington Bay Campground

TWO HARBORS

2.6 (2.8) Silver Creek

SHT follows Silver Creek almost continuously for the next 1.9 miles. Look for big old white pine on the opposite bank.

4.3 (1.1) Silver Creek campsite

▲ Silver Creek Campsite

Tent pads: 6
Water: From Silver Creek
Setting: On Silver Creek
Previous campsite: 5.9 miles
Next campsite: 8.7 miles

After turning left (east) away from Silver Creek, SHT continues for 1.0 miles through mixed forest to trailhead parking lot.

5.4 (0.0) Co. Rd. 301 (Fors Rd.) trailhead parking lot

Lake County Road 301 to Castle Danger

6.3 miles

Section description: Lake Co. Rd. 301 (Fors Rd.) to Silver Creek Township Rd. 617 (West Castle Danger Rd.)

Access and parking: *Directions to beginning trailhead:* At Hwy. 61 milepost 28.5, turn left on Lake Co. Rd. 3 and go 2.0 miles. Turn left on Lake Co. Rd. 301 (Fors Rd.) and go 0.3 miles to trailhead parking lot on left. Overnight parking okay.

Facilities at starting trailhead: none

Designated campsites on this section: none

Synopsis: The trail runs from rolling valleys up to rocky, pine-studded ridgelines. The Encampment River is a scenic halfway point, while the stunted trees and expansive views to the east are reminiscent of a hike at timberline in the Rockies.

Mile-by-Mile Description

0.0 (6.3) Lake Co. Rd. 301 (Fors Rd.) parking lot
SHT heads easterly in aspen-fir woods, soon descending past big spruces to a branch of Silver Creek. It continues east through woods and overgrown field, soon coming to Lake Co. Rd. 3, lined with planted pines.

0.7 (5.6) Lake Co. Rd. 3
SHT crosses Lake Co. Rd. 3 at angle and soon crosses ATV trail, then descends steeply to bridge over Wilson Creek. A few big old yellow birches and a small grove of cedars enhance creek bottom. SHT then climbs back out to flat upland at edge of old field dotted with spruce and fir. It temporarily joins ATV trail at a dip, rising slightly in mixed woods with some ash and balsam poplar in wetter spots. A few young sugar maples add diversity as SHT approaches Silver Creek Township Rd. 613.

1.1 (5.2) Silver Creek Township Rd. 613 (Loop Rd.)
SHT crosses 613 and travels through mixed forest of ash, aspen, and alder, then climbs gradually, crossing road to radio communication tower, over rocky ridge and down through thick balsam, crossing old Beaver Bay Rd. and small creek before climbing steeply.

2.3 (4.0) Pine Ridge Overlook
SHT comes to Pine Ridge Overlook with views of Two Harbors area to west from a ridge of red pines and spruce. Trail then passes through private land, traveling along boundary lines through white pine and cedar. Hikers are asked to be respectful of owner's rights and stay on trail. No camping or fires on private land.

3.6 (2.7) Encampment River crossing
SHT descends to bridge crossing, climbs to top of ridge east of Encampment River, then continues along ridgeline with views of Silver Creek, Stewart, and Encampment River valleys. Dwarfed spruces and pines and mossy ground combine with wide view to give this section feel of hiking at timberline in high mountains.

4.3 (2.0) Red pine overlook
Wide view from a red-pine framed outcrop into valley below before SHT turns into forest and down into low, wet area. Trail continues into mixed maple forest. A scenic view (with a bench) across the Crow Creek valley includes pine-studded Wolf Rock. This is private land, so please stay on trail. Wooden steps lead steeply into creek gorge. Note visible flows of rock in cliffs of creek. A 40-foot footbridge crosses Crow Creek, then SHT climbs a talus slope. Watch for "Poison Ivy" sign along slope. Trail continues through birches, crosses Silver Creek Township Rd. 617, then skirts base of dramatic cliffs into parking lot.

6.3 (0.0) Silver Creek Township Rd. 617 (West Castle Danger Rd.) parking lot

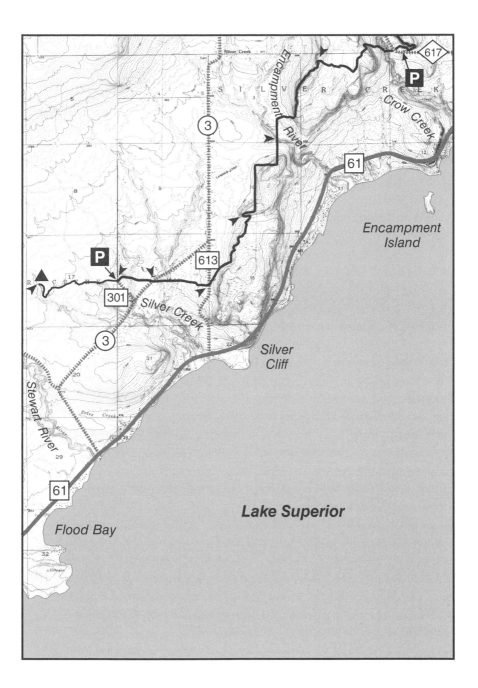

Castle Danger to Gooseberry Falls State Park
9.1 miles

Section description: Silver Creek Township Rd. 617 (West Castle Danger Rd.) to Gooseberry Falls State Park Visitor Center

Access and parking: *Directions to beginning trailhead:* At Hwy. 61 milepost 36.6, turn left on Lake Co. Rd. 106 (West Castle Danger Rd.) and go 0.6 miles. The road becomes Silver Creek Township Rd. 617. Continue another 1.8 miles to trailhead parking lot on right. Overnight parking okay.

Facilities at starting trailhead: none

Designated campsites on this section: five

Synopsis: This section starts with a short but steep climb to the ridgeline and Wolf Rock. It is the quickest way on any section of the trail to get to outstanding ridgeline views. After descending from the ridgeline and going through mixed forest, the trail ascends once more to Mike's Rock with more scenic vistas. The true highlight of the section is four miles of trail along the Gooseberry River, with its meandering course and a series of dramatic waterfalls.

Mile-by-Mile Description

0.0 (9.1) Silver Creek Township Road 617 parking lot
SHT departs right side of parking lot and climbs steeply through cliffs. This is one of the most dramatic first half-miles of the SHT as the trail winds up to top of Wolf Rock with its pine-clad rock outcrops.

0.5 (8.6) Wolf Rock
Great views at 1,200 feet of Lake Superior, Crow Creek valley, forests, etc. On ridge, SHT passes through mile of private land. Hikers are

asked to be respectful and stay on trail. No camping or fires on private land. Trail turns away from the valley as the woods alternate from open understory to dense growth. Decomposed lava looks like gravel on trailbed.

1.1 (8.0) Spur trail to overlook
The spur trail goes 215 yards to vista overlooking Crow Creek valley. SHT continues along ridge through a cedar grove that is the source of a stream, and up and down some rocky spots. The woods alternate from open understory to a dense growth enclosing the trail in a "green tunnel."

▲ Crow Creek Valley Campsite

Tent pads: 5
Water: From small stream, unreliable in dry conditions
Setting: In maple woods on small tributary of Crow Creek
Next campsite: 3.4 miles

2.9 (6.2) Mike's Rock
From Mike's Rock, there are vistas north and east to Gooseberry River Valley and Lake Superior. SHT descends stone steps past outcrops to low area of open birch and maple, crosses small stream and marshy area. Some dead birch in here, due to cumulative stress of drought, damage by birch leaf miner beetle and tent caterpillars.

4.0 (5.1) Nestor Grade crossing
This is an old logging railroad that was used for transporting logs to Lake Superior. SHT climbs to higher, drier ground and a beautiful stand of birch trees. Berry bushes abundant, including raspberry and thimbleberry. SHT crosses several intermittent streams and reaches overlook of Gooseberry River. Watch for signs of beavers along river.

4.7 (4.4) Gooseberry River and campsite
Note gravel bars along river—this is a good source of agates. SHT continues along river, with interesting meanders and oxbow cutoffs. The trail is subject to flooding in this area. These two miles of SHT

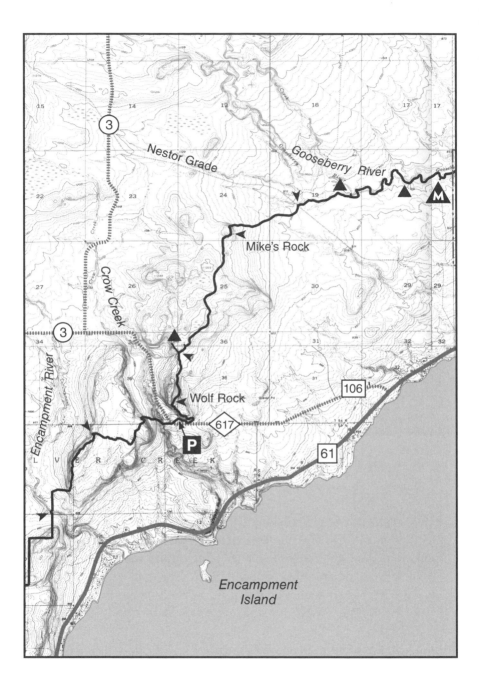

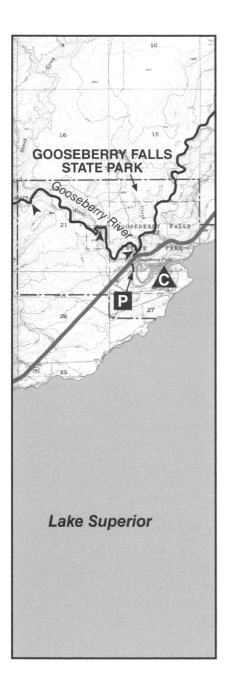

GOOSEBERRY FALLS
STATE PARK

Gooseberry River

Lake Superior

Gooseberry Falls State Park

Rocky Lake Superior shoreline and five waterfalls highlight Gooseberry Falls State Park. The park was established in 1933, and the Civilian Conservation Corps developed the park between 1934 and 1941, including the stone buildings, campground, picnic area, and trails. These structures have earned Gooseberry Falls State Park a place on the National Register of Historic Places. Today the park covers 1,675 acres and includes a 70-site drive-in campground, a rustic group camp at the former CCC camp location, and 18 miles of hiking trails (including a self-guided trail along the Gooseberry River). The Visitor Center at the wayside rest off of Highway 61 serves as an interpretive center and nature store. Its selection of quality outdoor education material is unsurpassed in the area. Interpretive programs are provided during the summer and include guided walks, activities, and evening programs.

are particularly beautiful in fall and mid-spring. There are many paths where beavers drag branches to water. Also, watch for migrating waterfowl in spring and fall.

▲ West Gooseberry Campsite

Tent pads: 4
Water: From Gooseberry River
Setting: On a hill above river
Previous campsite: 3.4 miles
Next campsite: 0.9 miles

▲ East Gooseberry Campsite

Tent pads: 2
Water: From Gooseberry River
Setting: On a small knoll close to river
Previous campsite: 0.9 miles
Next campsite: 4.0 miles

▲ Middle Gooseberry Campsite

Tent pads: 2
Water: From river
Setting: On river
Previous campsite: 0.4 miles
Next campsite: 0.4 miles

▲ Gooseberry River Multi-Group Campsite

Tent pads: 8
Water: From Gooseberry River
Setting: In a wooded area 30 yards from river
Previous campsite: 0.4 miles
Next campsite: 5.3 miles (or use Gooseberry Falls State
   Park Campground)

6.8 (2.3) Junction with park trail
Wide, grassy trail follows river for a distance, past shelter and up hill. Trail junction has arrows and "You are here" sign. Pass ten foot fence that protects young trees from deer damage, called a "deer exclosure." Trail makes sharp U-turn to left, descends to river and crosses bridge at Fifth Falls.

8.0 (1.1) Fifth Falls Bridge
After crossing river SHT follows park's Fifth Falls Trail along east side of Gooseberry River.

8.9 (0.2) Junction with spur trail
Main SHT turns sharply to left just before the old Visitor Center (stone building) and heads northeast to Split Rock River on wide ski trail.

To go from here to Visitor Center and parking lot, turn right, go past old Visitor Center, continue on paved trail, and take pedestrian bridge over Gooseberry River. Continue on to Visitor Center and parking lot.

Berries of the Superior Hiking Trail

Many hikers indulge in the satisfying experience of eating as they hike along the Superior Hiking Trail. Several species of berries are common along the trail, and they ripen from July to September. Blueberries are frequent on the rocky outcrops and scenic overlooks. These, as well as other sweet fruit species, need the full sun that is available on the hill crests. But don't limit your foraging to blueberries; keep your eyes peeled for strawberries, raspberries, thimbleberries, and juneberries. Bring along a bag or bucket— and remember, some berries are poisonous so eat only fruit that you know.

9.1 (0.0) Gooseberry Falls State Park Visitor Center

Gooseberry Falls State Park to Split Rock River Wayside
6.0 miles

Section description: Gooseberry Falls State Park Visitor Center to Split Rock River Wayside on Hwy. 61

Access and parking: *Directions to beginning trailhead:* At Hwy. 61 milepost 38.9, turn right and go 0.2 miles to Visitor Center parking lot for day use parking with no state park sticker required. For overnight parking, check in at contact station for campground to be directed to parking area. State park sticker required for overnight parking.

Facilities at starting trailhead: bathrooms, snacks, telephone, drinking water

Designated campsites on this section: one

Synopsis: This section starts out traveling through a variety of forests. The trail then climbs to and follows Bread Loaf Ridge with stunning views of Lake Superior making this section one of the best views on the SHT. The descent into the Split Rock River Valley is also quite spectacular.

Mile-by-Mile Description

0.0 (6.0) Gooseberry Falls State Park Visitor Center
Spur trail follows state park trail on pedestrian bridge across Gooseberry River and past old visitors center, where it intersects main SHT. Main SHT veers right onto ski trails. SHT travels through birch and pine, up a high rise and across Nelson's Creek. The trail is well marked at junctions with other ski trails. SHT leaves ski trail and continues on hiking trail to state park boundary.

1.2 (4.8) SHT sign
SHT goes through aspen, birch, and cedar, and then gently descends, leveling out in cedar grove. A sign notes contribution of Philip

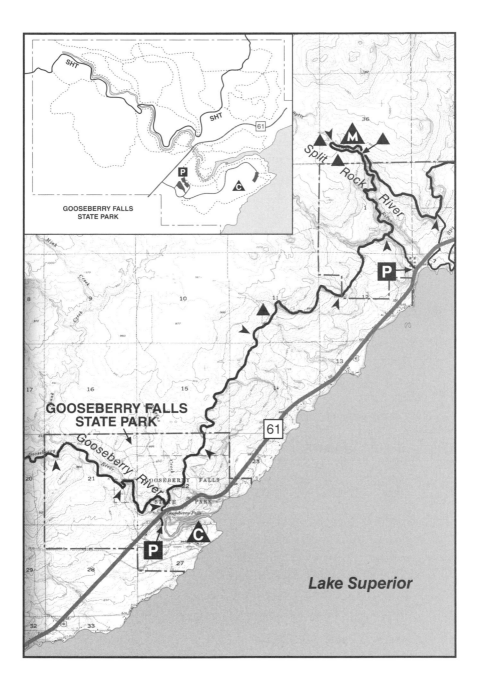

GOOSEBERRY FALLS
STATE PARK

GOOSEBERRY FALLS
STATE PARK

Lake Superior

Economon family. SHT follows base of ridge through lovely birch forest and crosses five small footbridges across creeks. Trail travels through nice stand of white pines.

2.8 (3.2) Blueberry Hill Rd.

SHT crosses dirt road, goes through birch and poplar, crosses bridge, passes campsite, then climbs small hill to cedar grove.

▲ Blueberry Hill Campsite

Tent pads: 4
Water: From creek at campsite behind fire ring; unreliable in dry conditions
Setting: In birch woods
Previous campsite: 5.3 miles (or use Gooseberry Falls State Park)
Next campsite: 4.0 miles

3.4 (2.6) Bread Loaf Ridge

After a short but steep climb marked by two arrow signs, SHT comes out onto ridge with stunning overlook of Lake Superior and forest. The ridge, with weathered rock, reindeer lichen, and wild roses, continues for almost a mile. Rock cairns mark trail in rocky areas. Trail descends into Split Rock River valley. It continues up a steep grade into Split Rock Lighthouse State Park (note sign) and then follows an easy descent through beautiful birch groves. Trail passes by top of waterfall on branch of Split Rock River.

5.5 (0.5) Waterfall and trail junction

At junction, go left to continue on main SHT along Split Rock River Loop or right on spur trail 0.5 miles to Hwy. 61 trailhead parking lot.

6.0 (0.0) Split Rock River Wayside on Hwy. 61

Public-Private Cooperation

We take things for granted sometimes—like a clearly marked trail, or a footbridge over a low wet area. In fact, some things we almost can't help but take for granted because we never learn about them. For example, private landowners have helped make the Superior Hiking Trail a reality by sharing their property. More than 10% of the trail crosses land that is privately owned. Less than 1% crosses property of the Superior Hiking Trail Association. As you hike the trail, please remember that you are often a guest!

Split Rock River Loop
5.0 miles

Section description: Section begins and ends at Split Rock River Wayside

Access and parking: *Directions to beginning trailhead:* At Hwy. 61 milepost 43.5 on left side of highway for day use only. For overnight parking, go to Split Rock Light State Park main entrance at Hwy. 61 milepost 49.0. Turn right on entrance road and check in at Visitor Center to be directed to parking area. State park sticker required for overnight parking. Follow state park trails marked with SHT logos and white blazes 2.3 miles to Split Rock River Loop.

Facilities at starting trailhead: none

Designated campsites on this section: four

Synopsis: This is one of the premier day-hike loops on the SHT. The attractive trail ascends the west side of the river, which cascades down past cliffs and through clefts of sheer red rock walls draped with conifers to Lake Superior. After crossing the river, the trail affords some beautiful views along the river. The trail then leaves the river and goes through forest until reaching a park shelter with a commanding overlook of Lake Superior and the river valley.

Mile-by-Mile Description

0.0 (5.0) Split Rock River Wayside
0.5 mile spur to main trail climbs gradually, with views of river valley to the east.

0.5 (4.5) Junction with SHT
Watch for sharp right turn from spur trail to main trail. SHT descends steeply to gorgeous waterfall on branch of Split Rock River. Trail becomes more difficult climbing steep hills. Watch for washouts and

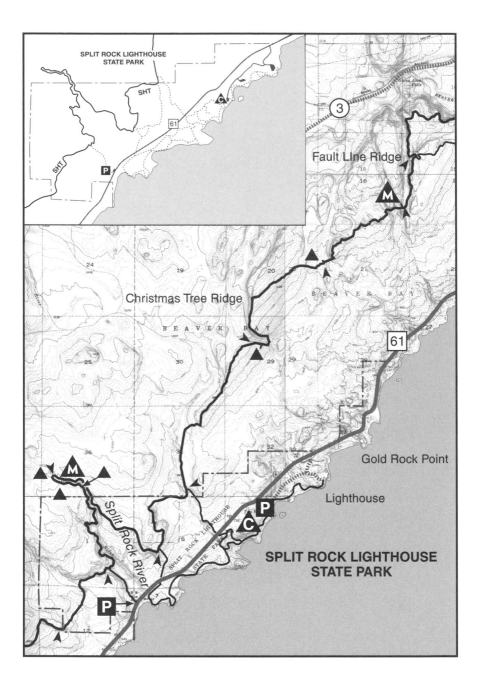

exposed tree roots. Trail winds through impressive rock formations, including chimney formation known as the Pillars. Many waterfalls are passed along the way. Watch for large rock outcrop in middle of river that splits flow of river around a tree-studded island.

▲ Southwest Split Rock River Campsite

Tent pads: 4
Water: From Split Rock River
Setting: 0.5 miles from footbridge, on west side of river
Previous campsite: 4.0 miles
Next campsite: 0.4 miles

▲ Northwest Split Rock River Campsite

Tent pads: 3
Water: From Split Rock River
Setting: Right before footbridge on west side of river, in a grove of cedar trees on a small hill
Previous campsite: 0.4 miles
Next campsite: 0.2 miles

2.6 (2.4) Split Rock River crossing

SHT crosses Split Rock River on bridge and travels by conifers and bare rock outcrops. River cascades through red rock canyon walls topped with conifers.

▲ Northeast Split Rock River Campsite

Tent pads: 7
Water: From Split Rock River
Setting: 0.3 miles south of footbridge on east side of river, in grove of large aspen trees
Previous campsite: 0.2 miles
Next campsite: 0.3 miles

Geology of Split Rock River

The reddish-tan color of the rock in the Split Rock River gorge is quite a contrast to the more typical dark gray to black colors of the basalts of the North Shore. This rock, known as rhyolite, formed from a massive lava flow. As the flow cooled, it developed vertical cracks, or "columnar joints," similar to those at Palisade Head, as well as many smaller horizontal cracks. Postglacial river erosion of the last 11,000 years, made easy by all these fractures, has eaten deeply into the flow, but has left some columns isolated right alongside the trail. Frost action over the centuries produces the "shingle" effect of loose chips and slabs on the rock surface and along the trail.

▲ Southeast Split Rock River Campsite

Tent pads: 2
Water: From Split Rock River
Setting: 0.6 miles south of footbridge on east side of river, across from the stone pillars
Previous campsite: 0.3 miles
Next campsite: 4.7 miles

After campsite, trail reaches wide overlook, with view of Lake Superior and lighthouse. Day use shelter marks junction with state park ski trails.

4.3 (0.7) Junction with spur trail to Hwy. 61

At junction with spur trail by sign, SHT spur trail turns right and descends steeply back to Hwy. 61 on park ski trail. SHT spur turns right at Hwy. 61 and goes along path by ditch and then inside guardrail for 200 yards to wayside parking lot.

5.0 (0.0) Hwy. 61 parking lot

Split Rock River Wayside to Beaver Bay

11.3 miles

Section description: Split Rock River Wayside or Split Rock Lighthouse State Park to Lake Co. Rd. 4 (Lax Lake Rd.) north of Beaver Bay

Access and parking: *There are two beginning trailheads:*

1) Split Rock River Wayside. At Hwy. 61 milepost 43.5 on left side of highway for day use only. Walk from parking lot 200 yards northeast to start of SHT spur trail going to main SHT.

2) Split Rock Lighthouse State Park. At Hwy. 61 milepost 49.0, turn right on entrance road and follow directions to parking. State park sticker required. Follow state park trails marked with SHT logos and white blazes 2.3 miles to SHT spur trail going to main SHT. Overnight parking okay with state park sticker.

Facilities at starting trailhead: none. Services available at Split Rock Lighthouse State Park: bathrooms, water, phone.

Designated campsites on this section: three

Synopsis: A challenging rocky trail affording dramatic views both of Lake Superior and inland. In many places the SHT follows along the edge of high escarpments with conifers clinging precariously 300 to 400 feet above the valley floor. There are many steep ascents and descents that take one through a wide variety of forests—much birch, maple, and aspen as well as impressive stands of cedars and white pines. The section also traverses part of the Merrill Grade, one of the historic logging railroads. Many sections of the SHT traverse long ridges of table rock, or follow long outcroppings that form walkways for the SHT. In one area hikers must proceed carefully along a pond bounded with large rocks and small boulders. There is also a 6.0-mile loop from Cove Point Lodge in the middle of this section.

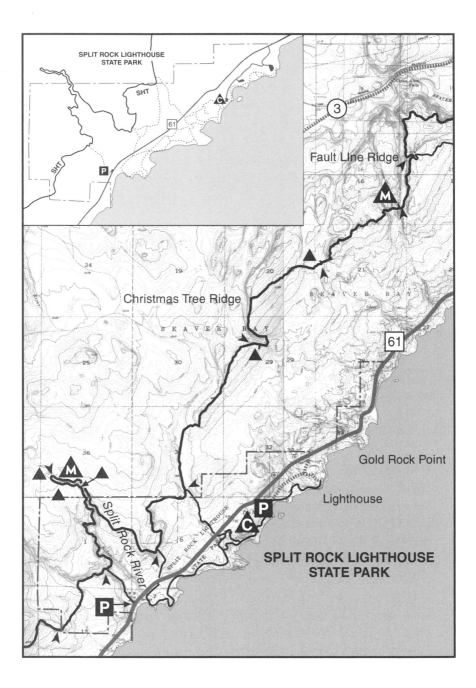

SPLIT ROCK LIGHTHOUSE
STATE PARK

Fault Line Ridge

Christmas Tree Ridge

Gold Rock Point

Lighthouse

BEAVER
BAY

Cove Point

61

Lake Superior

Split Rock Lighthouse State Park

Established as a park in 1971, today Split Rock Lighthouse State Park includes 2,075 acres along Lake Superior between the Split Rock River and the lighthouse. The park hosts a number of historic sites including a commercial fishing village site, an early mine site, the site of a logging camp and dam, and of course the lighthouse and surrounding buildings. One of the unique aspects of the park is the cart-in campground. Campers cart in rather than drive in to the 20 sites located along Lake Superior. Four lakeside backpack sites are also available. Twelve miles of trails connect and follow the lakeshore and the ridge 600 feet above. Another popular pastime, fishing, especially for trout and salmon, is excellent along the Split Rock River.

Mile-by-Mile Description

0.0 (11.3) Split Rock River Wayside
From parking lot, walk northeast along Hwy. 61 behind guardrail and on trail in ditch for 200 yards to 0.5-mile spur trail on left that climbs steeply to main SHT at junction marked by directional sign.

0.5 (10.8) Junction with SHT
From junction, SHT goes right to head towards Beaver Bay. Trail follows ridgeline, passing two good vistas of Lake Superior and lighthouse, then descends. Some of rock outcrops are old shorelines of Glacial Lake Duluth. The long gentle descent leads to a low, boggy area, then the junction with a ski trail, then a wide ski trail bridge over Split Rock Creek.

1.7 (9.6) Junction with spur to state park
Soon after crossing creek, there is a 1.4-mile spur from state park on right. SHT soon travels on old Merrill Grade railroad route. Trail follows moss-covered remains of old railroad ties through birch, aspen, and balsam. Watch for sign where SHT departs grade. Trail climbs to long walk along exposed rock ridge with spruce and lichen-covered rocks and steep drops to north. SHT crosses ATV trail at 3.0 miles. Note the beautiful large pines along the trail.

3.4 (7.9) Chapins Ridge Campsite

▲ Chapins Ridge Campsite
Tent pads: 4
Water: 0.2 miles away at Chapins Creek beaver pond, unreliable in dry conditions
Setting: In grove of white pine trees
Previous campsite: 4.7 miles
Next campsite: 2.2 miles

Just past campsite, SHT follows 30-foot wooden stairway and crosses beaver pond on bridge. SHT crosses logging road, then climbs to overlook atop Christmas Tree Ridge through open grassy area with good views inland. Trail continues in open area, through a fine stand of white pines, and descends from ridge through brush and aspen, and past another beaver pond.

5.6 (5.7) Beaver pond Campsite

▲ Beaver Pond Campsite

Tent pads: 4
Water: From beaver pond
Setting: On beaver pond
Previous campsite: 2.2 miles
Next campsite: 1.5 miles

SHT passes beaver pond and then climbs sharply to vistas north and west. Trail follows rock promontories in a series of short ascents and descents. From ridge SHT descends steeply into valley and wetter area.

7.1 (4.2) Fault Line Creek Campsite

▲ Fault Line Creek Campsite

Tent pads: 8
Water: From beaver pond
Setting: On shore of large beaver pond
Previous campsite: 1.5 miles
Next campsite: 4.35 miles

History of Split Rock Lighthouse

For a few centuries now, people have been trying to move safely along the North Shore of Lake Superior. Split Rock Lighthouse, which is visible from a number of points along the SHT, was one of many efforts to make the trip easier. Built in response to a particularly tragic year of shipwrecks (1905, with 215 lives lost on the lake), the lighthouse operated from 1910 to 1961. The light was visible up to 60 miles away. Today, the lighthouse is operated by the Minnesota Historial Society and is one of the most popular tourist sites on the North Shore, with over 200,000 visitors a year.

After campsite on large beaver pond, SHT crosses Fault Line Creek, passes high mound of giant boulders, then follows rocky shore of beaver pond. Trail climbs steeply through birch forest to Fault Line Ridge, formed by a geologic fault. Trail proceeds along east rim of fault valley, with dramatic views into deep valley.

7.6 (3.7) Junction with west Cove Point spur

At a major break in Fault Line Ridge, spur trail on right leads to Cove Point Lodge, on Lake Superior shore (see sidebar). Main SHT

Cove Point Spur Trail Loop

This loop section was built in 1996 with assistance from volunteers provided by Cove Point Lodge. With a little less than three new miles of trail a great six-mile loop was created, including the dramatic cliffs above the Beaver River and at the Fault Line Ridge.

The SHT spur begins just above the Cove Point Lodge parking lot, crosses Highway 61 and continues uphill, crossing a stream and passing through a former mink farm. After passing a communications tower, the spur trail comes to the junction at 1.2 miles.

The eastern spur leads about a half mile through birch forest to two hills, the second with a dramatic overlook of Lake Superior and the interior. This was previously a dead end overlook of the original SHT.

The eastern spur continues on the main SHT 1.8 miles to the western spur. This section of the SHT passes the Beaver River overlook cliffs and Fault Line Ridge overlooks with their numerous red pines.

The western spur is longer, 1.1 miles. It heads back to Cove Point from the SHT at a major break in Fault Line Ridge. The western spur ascends a steep rocky staircase, then follows the rim of a gorge to the left. Several small rises are encountered. After crossing and following a stream the western spur meets the eastern spur at the junction back to Cove Point Lodge.

continues along ridgeline, then after one last overlook turns east and follows cliffs above Beaver River. Views include railroad tracks linking the taconite mines of Babbitt with the processing plant in Silver Bay. Hikers can hear, and with leaves off see, Glen Avon Falls on the Beaver River.

9.4 (1.9) Junction with east Cove Point spur
Spur trail on right goes 200 yards to view of Lake Superior or continues down to shore. Main SHT continues towards Co. Rd. 4 through birch, maple, and balsam forests, with groves of cedar in some low areas. Trail crosses snowmobile trail 30 yards before Co. Rd. 4.

11.3 (0.0) Co. Rd. 4 trailhead parking lot

Beaver Bay to Silver Bay
4.7 miles

Section description: Lake Co. Rd. 4 (Lax Lake Rd.) to Lake Co. Rd. 5 (Penn Blvd.)

Access and parking: *Directions to beginning trailhead:* At Hwy. 61 milepost 51.1, turn left on Lake Co. Rd. 4 (Lax Lake Rd.) and go 0.8 miles to trailhead parking lot on right. Overnight parking okay.

Facilities at starting trailhead: none

Designated campsites on this section: two

Synopsis: This section of trail follows the lovely Beaver River with its gorgeous falls for over a half mile before turning away from the river and then climbing a high ridge studded with pines. The trail continues along the ridge with dramatic views of the Beaver River valley. After descending to cross the Silver Bay Golf Course Road, the trail again climbs to the ridgeline with many challenging ascents and descents, traveling on rocky outcrops and affording stunning views of Lake Superior.

Mile-by-Mile Description

0.0 (4.7) Lake Co. Rd. 4 parking lot
SHT leaves lot sharing snowmobile/ATV trail and after 0.5 miles crosses Beaver River on a metal bridge. SHT turns right immediately after bridge and goes along river. This scenic river walk passes groves of cedar and white pine, following river as it changes from a gentle wide river to a roaring cascade.

Minnesota's Taconite Industry

Since the 1950s, the history and landscape of the Beaver Bay area have been tied to the processing and shipping of taconite, a low-grade iron ore found naturally in deposits 50 miles inland. Reserve Mining Company built the world's first large taconite concentrating and pelletizing plant, creating the company town of Silver Bay. In the 1970s Reserve Mining drew criticism for its practice of dumping many thousands of tons of taconite tailings into Lake Superior daily. Following a 1978 federal court ruling, Reserve built the immense Milepost 7 tailings pond a few miles behind Beaver Bay. The tailings sludge is pumped through huge pipes from the Silver Bay plant. Reserve Mining Co. closed its Babbitt mine and Silver Bay plant in 1986. In 1989, Cyprus Minerals Company bought the plant and reopened it on a smaller scale. Since 1994, Northshore Mining has been a subsidiary of Cleveland Cliffs.

▲ North Beaver River Campsite

Tent pads: 3
Water: From Beaver River
Setting: On Beaver River
Previous campsite: 4.35 miles
Next campsite: .25 miles

▲ South Beaver River Campsite

Tent pads: 3
Water: From Beaver River
Setting: On Beaver River
Previous campsite: .25 miles
Next campsite: 5.8 miles

After campsites, SHT turns away from river and climbs through cedar, spruce, and birch to old Betzler Rd. SHT turns left (north) at road.

1.1 (3.6) Railroad tracks crossing
SHT follows Betzler Rd. crossing main railroad line bringing taconite to Silver Bay for processing from mine in Babbitt. SHT follows Betzler Rd. for another 100 yards, then angles right into balsam thicket, then up through fragrant stand of red and white pines to Sulheim's Overlook, with a view of ridges, forest, and far in distance the tailings basin. Trail continues along cliff edge with view of tailings ponds and pumping station.

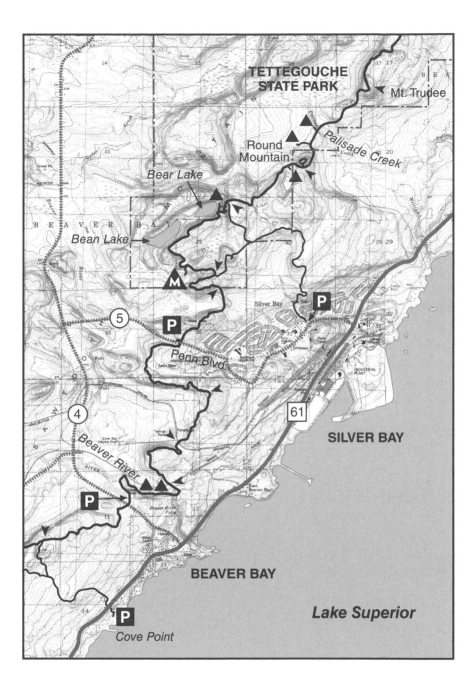

TETTEGOUCHE
STATE PARK

Mt. Trudee

Palisade Creek

Round
Mountain

Bear Lake

Bean Lake

B E A V E R   B A Y

M

P

5

P

Penn Blvd

Silver Bay

P

4

Beaver River

RIVER

61

SILVER BAY

P

BEAVER BAY

Lake Superior

P

Cove Point

2.2 (2.5) Golf Course Rd. crossing

SHT comes out onto a snowmobile/ATV trail and follows it for 20 yards, crosses the Silver Bay Golf Course Road, and then follows the snowmobile/ATV trail for another 25 yards. SHT leaves snowmobile/ATV on right and goes uphill in stand of aspens. SHT then leads gradually uphill to overlook amidst red pines with views of Lake Superior. As visible from overlook, forest here is sea of birches with occasional towering white and red pines. SHT continues through this forest, up ridgeline, across ATV trail and then up rocky open ridgeline.

3.2 (1.5) View of Silver Bay, Northshore Mining plant

SHT follows ridge overlooking Silver Bay. Note unusual clumps of low, leafy bearberry and juniper. SHT winds along first ridge, then descends and climbs again to a second ridge, called "Blueberry Ridge" by the locals. From a clump of red pines one can look back to parking lot on Co. Rd. 4 where the hike began. Beaver pond below may provide an opportunity for watching beavers at work. SHT descends into mixed woods, past a trail, through a wet area with ash trees, then gently up one final rocky ridge before crossing a snowmobile trail and crossing Penn Blvd. to parking lot.

4.7 (0.0) Penn Blvd. trailhead parking lot

Silver Bay to Tettegouche State Park and Highway 1

11.1 miles

Section description: Lake Co. Rd. 5 (Penn Blvd.) to State Hwy. 1

Access and parking: *Directions to beginning trailhead:* At Hwy. 61 milepost 54.3, turn left at stoplight on Outer Driver and go 1.5 miles to Penn Blvd. Continue straight 0.5 miles on Penn Blvd. to trailhead parking lot on right. Overnight parking okay.

There are two additional parking options for this section: 1) Tettegouche State Park Wayside at Hwy. 61, milepost 58.5 on right with no state park sticker required. For this option, take the state park spur trail after the bridge on the High Falls of the Baptism River down to the wayside. Total mileage for this option is 11.7 miles.

2) At the state park trailhead parking lot inside the state park with a state park sticker required, also located at Hwy. 61 milepost 58.5 on right. Total mileage for this option is 10.0 miles.

Facilities at starting trailhead: none

Designated campsites on this section: five

Synopsis: This is one of the more challenging sections of the SHT, with lots of up and down, great views of Lake Superior and inland bluffs. It begins in the outskirts of Silver Bay and winds past beautiful Bean and Bear Lakes in Tettegouche State Park. The trail continues through Tettegouche past Round Mountain and Mt. Trudee with fantastic views and by the backcountry "gem lakes." The highlight of the section is the dramatic High Falls on the Baptism River.

Twin Lakes (Bean and Bear Lakes) Loop Option: Starting from the Penn Blvd. trailhead, there is a 6.8 mile loop that ends back at the same trailhead. This loop climbs and descends three ridges in predominantly maple forests and views the picturesque Bean and Bear Lakes. This

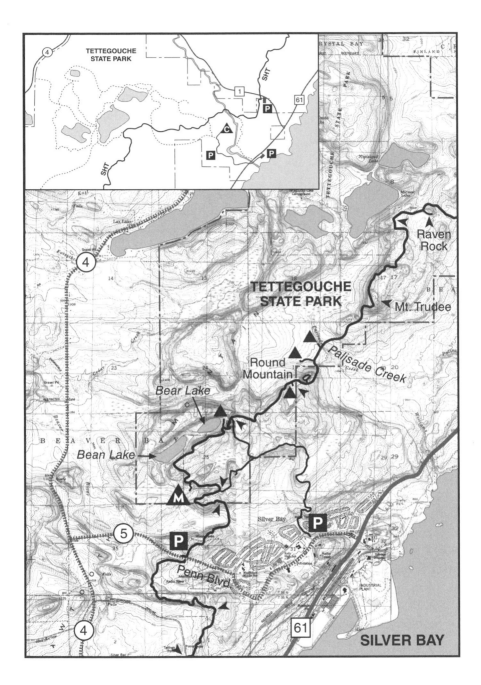

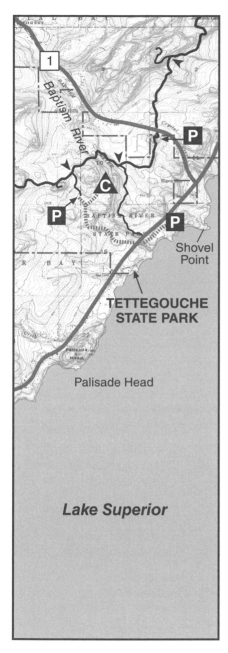

loop can also be started from the Silver Bay Visitor Center on Outer Drive 0.5 miles from Hwy. 61 on right with a total loop mileage of 7.6 miles (see sidebar on page 125).

Mile-by-Mile Description

0.0 (11.1) Penn Blvd.

SHT departs parking lot on short spur shared with snow-mobiles/ATVs for 100 yards to main SHT. Main SHT turns left at sign and goes uphill. Trail crosses ATV trail, passes a sumac stand, crosses a gravel road (to Silver Bay's water supply), and then passes under powerline into spruce trees. SHT then ascends ridgeline and crosses another ATV trail.

1.0 (10.1) Series of outcrops with south and west views

SHT comes to views over Silver Bay, water tower, Northshore Mining plant, and Lake Superior. In another 0.3 miles, there is a nice view of an oak-maple-birch ridge.

1.8 (9.3) Junction with Twin Lakes Trail

SHT comes to first of two junctions with the Twin Lakes Trail. Trail crosses footbridge on Penn Creek, enters forest with maples dominating the low portion of the south-facing slope, then passes outcrops with oak and sumac. Lots of blueberries and juneberries in this area. At one outcrop you can see back to previous outcrop and beaver pond before trail descends.

⚠ Penn Creek Campsite

Tent pads: 8
Water: From Penn Creek, unreliable in dry conditions
Setting: In woods
Previous campsite: 5.8 miles
Next campsite: 1.4 miles

2.6 (8.5) Bean Lake overlook
From overlook Mt. Trudee is visible to east, marked by dark red pines and flat top. SHT travels length of Bean and Bear Lakes on high cliffs looking down on the sparkling lakes far below.

3.4 (7.7) Bear Lake Campsite
The 150-yard spur trail to the campsite at Bear Lake is on left and descends sharply to lake.

▲ Bear Lake Campsite

Tent pads: 4
Water: From Bear Lake
Setting: 150 yards off SHT on steep spur trail, on shore of Bear Lake
Previous campsite: 1.4 miles
Next campsite: 1.2 miles

3.6 (7.5) Eastern junction with Twin Lakes Trail
At top of bluff, SHT comes to next junction with Twin Lakes Trail on right marked with sign. SHT continues through level maple-birch woods, drops to overlook of valley and view of Round Mountain and Mt. Trudee and descends to beaver pond.

▲ Round Mountain Beaver Pond Campsite

Tent pads: 6
Water: From beaver pond
Setting: 0.1 miles west of Round Mountain spur, on pond
Previous campsite: 1.2 miles
Next campsite: 0.8 mile

4.8 (6.3) Spur trail up Round Mountain

0.25-mile spur trail to dramatic overlook of Palisade Creek Valley. SHT passes mature sugar maple forest and descends into Palisade Creek Valley, crossing ATV trail, two foot bridges and wet area with white cedars. SHT crosses West Palisade Creek and comes to 300-yard spur trail to campsite on left. Trail then passes East Palisade Creek campsite and descends to bridge over East Palisade Creek. SHT crosses ATV trail and then climbs a series of wooden steps through mixed woods to stunning views.

▲ West Palisade Creek Campsite

Tent pads: 5
Water: From West Palisade Creek
Setting: 1.0 miles west of Mt. Trudee, on creek
Previous campsite: 0.8 miles
Next campsite: 0.2 miles

▲ East Palisade Creek Campsite

Tent pads: 4
Water: From East Palisade Creek
Setting: 0.8 miles west of Mt. Trudee, on creek
Previous campsite: 0.2 miles
Next campsite: 7.8 miles (or use Tettegouche State Park)

Twin Lakes Trail

How about a walk through town? When the town is nestled in the wilderness like Silver Bay, that can be quite a trek. The Twin Lakes Trail, named after the dramatic Bean and Bear Lakes, is a 7.6 mile "lollipop loop" that has a "stem" of 2.3 miles before the lake loop.

The trail starts as an ATV trail at the Bay Area Historical Society parking lot in Silver Bay. Watch for the distinctive Twin Lakes Trail signs. It crosses Banks Blvd., then continues up a hill and a very nice little hogback area. After 0.7 miles on the ATV trail, watch for a spur trail on the right. The loop junction is another 1.6 miles. Watch for signs.

Tettegouche State Park

Tettegouche State Park was established in 1979, and contains 9,346 acres of land, including six inland lakes and one mile of Lake Superior shoreline. Flowing through the park is the Baptism River and on it, High Falls, the highest falls completely in Minnesota. At the southeast corner of the park lies Palisade Head, a high bluff with a sheer rock face falling 200 feet into Lake Superior below. The park has 34 campsites. The rugged, semi-mountainous terrain, and spectacular overlooks, make hiking on the park's seventeen miles of trails very popular. A one-mile self-guided trail to Shovel Point along Lake Superior educates as well as inspires. For the history buff, there is the Tettegouche Camp, a 1910 social camp. Its log buildings have been restored for overnight rentals. In addition, there is rich logging, maple syruping, and mining history throughout the park.

6.3 (4.8) Mt. Trudee
Mt. Trudee offers one of SHT's best examples of a large, weather-resistant anorthosite dome. Its summit is picturesque, studded with pines, with great views. SHT continues along top of Trudee, with views including Tettegouche and Mic Mac Lakes (named after lakes in Labrador, Canada), then descends through maple forest. Forest changes to mixed maple-birch, starting at series of rock walls alongside trail.

7.5 (3.6) Junction with state park trail "L"
SHT comes to state park post with letter "L." SHT turns right on state park trail, first through pure maples, then through low area and copse of white cedars. A spur trail leads to good views from Raven Rock.

8.2 (2.9) Junction with state park trail "C"
SHT comes to state park post with letter "C" and continues straight. SHT descends through mixed maple-birch-conifer forest, past 12-foot circumference white pine, then through "The Drainpipe," a 150-foot rock crevice with rock steps. SHT crosses another ski trail and travels through white cedar lowland.

9.7 (1.4) Junction "B" with access trail to Tettegouche State Park trailhead parking lot

SHT comes to state park post with letter "B." To access Tettegouche parking lot, turn right and go 0.3 miles downhill to parking lot, through white pine grove, passing state park post "A." Main SHT continues through mature birch, across plank walkways. Watch for spur trail to state park campground. Main SHT descends wooden stairs, passes Baptism High Falls overlook, then crosses Baptism River on suspension bridge just above falls. These are the highest falls entirely in Minnesota. The bridge, built in 1991 with substantial help from Minnesota Power, has a unique single-cable suspension design. This was by far the most elaborate and expensive bridge built by SHTA. At trailside bench on other side of river, look for spur trail to base of High Falls. SHT leaves river and goes up wood staircase.

Sugar Maple Forests

The extensive maple forests of the SHT, which create much of the gorgeous colors of a fall hike, are the result of a lucky combination of ecological factors. Sugar maples require relatively warm winters and fairly deep soil to survive, both of which are rare in northern Minnesota. Maples can't survive below -40 °. The thermal mass of Lake Superior keeps the north shore cool in the summer, but also keeps the area warm in winter. Maples thrive on the ridgelines, but not in the adjacent valleys, into which cold air sinks. The maple forests get their deep soil as a gift from two different glaciers which advanced parallel to each other, on both sides of the ridgeline, leaving enough glacial till on the ridges for this beautiful, out-of-place forest to thrive.

10.4 (0.7) Junction with state park trail

Spur trail follows river downstream 1.3 miles to park visitor center and wayside rest. Main SHT goes into birch woods and passes two large white pines, followed by a balsam fir "tunnel." SHT heads through cedars, up hill and along ridge, then climbs 100-yard rock staircase. Large rock amphitheater is former quarry site, the first quarry used in early days of 3M Company. Spur trail leads to SHT parking lot on Hwy. 1.

11.1 (0.0) State Hwy. 1 trailhead parking lot

Highway 1 to Lake County Road 6
6.8 miles

Section description: State Hwy. 1 to Lake Co. Rd. 6

Access and parking: *Directions to beginning trailhead:* At Hwy. 61 milepost 59.3, turn left on Hwy. 1 and go 0.8 miles to trailhead parking lot on left. Watch closely as this lot is easy to miss. Overnight parking okay.

Facilities at starting trailhead: none

Designated campsites on this section: two

Synopsis: This section varies greatly from easy, long stretches along the contours to steep, scrambling ascents and descents. There are many open ledges affording beautiful views of both Lake Superior and its shoreline, and inland lakes, mountains and valleys. The trail winds through pockets of maples.

Mile-by-Mile Description

0.0 (6.8) State Hwy. 1 parking lot
From parking lot, short SHT spur trail goes uphill to main SHT. Main SHT turns right, crosses Hwy. 1 and continues through forest, crosses Crystal Creek, and enters a 1990 burned area of birch and aspen, marked with a sign. Trail crosses gravel logging road and traverses wet area with Sawtooth Mtn. summits ahead. Trail soon climbs steeply to ridgeline.

0.9 (5.9) Spur trail to Fantasia Overlook
SHT comes to 0.5-mile spur trail to Fantasia Overlook with views of Lake Superior, Palisade Head, Mt. Trudee, and the Silver Bay Harbor. Below are views of vertical cliffs and beaver pond. Main SHT continues downhill from the overlook trail, levels out in valley where it briefly shares

an old road, then rises sharply to open ledges with view of Lake Superior. Trail turns away from lake, descends a bit, and then climbs switchbacks to an overlook above Wolf Lake, a beautiful lake deep in a depression. From overlook, trail curves around peak, descends, then climbs again to ridgeline overlooking Lake Superior.

2.3 (4.5) Kennedy Creek Campsites
SHT heads back into woods to campsites. Between campsites, SHT continues across bridge and passes 0.25 mile spur trail that goes to Wolf Ridge Environmental Learning Center and Raven Lake. SHT climbs to a small dome and descends again.

▲ West Kennedy Creek Campsite

Tent pads: 5
Water: From Kennedy Creek, unreliable in dry conditions
Setting: In wooded area
Previous campsite: 7.8 miles
Next campsite: 0.1 miles

▲ East Kennedy Creek Campsite

Tent pads: 4
Water: From Kennedy Creek, unreliable in dry conditions
Setting: In wooded area
Previous campsite: 0.1 miles
Next campsite: 5.8 miles

2.9 (3.9) Powerline
100 yards before powerline, SHT crosses old road. Trail continues and climbs to expansive view of Lake Superior, Fantasia, Mystical Mountain and Marshall Mountain. SHT follows a curving cliff line before it parallels Lake Superior on a high ridge, with fleeting glimpses of lake. Trail passes through two big rocks.

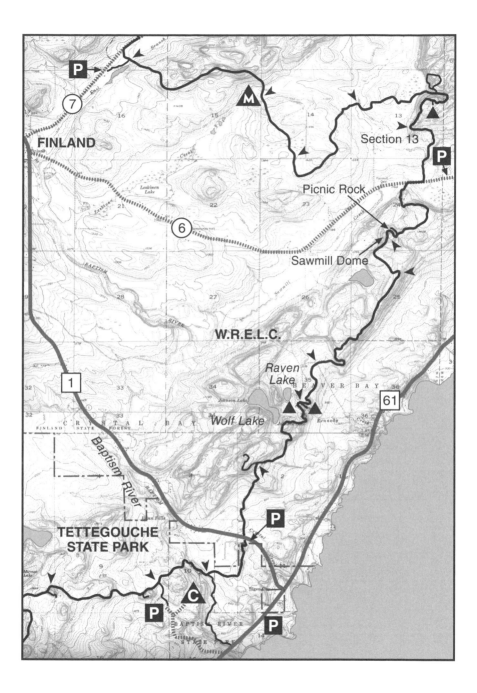

P

⑦

FINLAND

M

Section 13

P

Picnic Rock

⑥

Sawmill Dome

BAPTISM

W.R.E.L.C.

1

Raven
Lake

BEAVER BAY

Wolf Lake

61

Baptism River

TETTEGOUCHE
STATE PARK

P

C

P

P

Wolf Ridge Environmental Learning Center

The Wolf Ridge Environmental Learning Center (WRELC) facility is a cluster of buildings with 1000 acres of surrounding land that accommodates hundreds of students, both youth and adult. Wolf Ridge has been at its current site since 1988, though the program started in Isabella, Minnesota, in the early 1970s. The well-regarded residential environmental education program has introduced over a quarter-million students to the wonders of the north woods; weekend programs offer a wide variety of experiences for adults and families. The trails on the WRELC intersect with the SHT, allowing for excursions onto the SHT from the WRELC parking lot. Look for the Wolf Ridge turnoff a few miles up Lake Co. Rd. 6.

4.7 (2.1) Overlook

From overlook, SHT turns sharply inland towards Sawmill Dome and remains level through maple woods until last rise to top of Sawmill Dome. This large cliff is studded with large pines and overlooks a maple forest, farmsteads, and buildings of Wolf Ridge ELC. Sawmill Dome and Sawmill Creek in valley below are named after turn-of-the-century Warren Sawmill in Little Marais.

6.0 (0.8) Sawmill Dome

SHT skirts Sawmill Dome with steep cliffs, then descends sharply, past spur trail to Picnic Rock, which goes 150 yards to a semi-cave at base of cliffs. SHT continues to overlook of Sawmill Creek valley, old Air Force radar base, and Co. Rd. 6, then descends. The trail climbs briefly up log and rock steps to hilltop with views of Lake Superior and ridgeline. It then descends past stone steps and wildlife opening.

6.8 (0.0) Lake Co. Rd. 6 parking area

Parking lot is 0.4 miles right (east) on Co. Rd. 6 in gravel pit. Main SHT continues on other side of road after 0.2 miles.

Lake County Road 6 to Finland Recreation Center
7.6 miles

Section description: Lake Co. Rd. 6 to Finland Recreation Center on Lake Co. Rd. 7 (Cramer Rd.)

Access and parking: *Directions to beginning trailhead:* At Hwy. 61 milepost 65.3, turn left on Lake Co. Rd. 6 and go 2.1 miles to trailhead parking lot in gravel pit on right. Trail starts 0.2 miles west along Co. Rd. 6. Overnight parking okay.

Facilities at starting trailhead: none

Designated campsites on this section: two

Synopsis: This hike leads to some of the most impressive terrain on the SHT, including the high cliffs overlooking the Sawmill Creek and Baptism River valleys, popular with local rock climbers and known as the Section 13 cliffs. There is an impressive boardwalk that has been constructed over a beaver dam and a huge rock, known as a glacial erratic, that is over 20 feet tall. This section passes through excellent moose habitat and the east branch of the Baptism River.

Mile-by-Mile Description

0.0 (7.6) Lake Co. Rd. 6
SHT departs from Co. Rd. 6 on right about 0.2 miles west of parking lot. Trail enters dark spruce and birch forest, then crosses boardwalk through wet areas. SHT crosses Sawmill Creek and then another small creek. Trail climbs gradually along fir- and spruce-lined ridge, past beaver pond. At first there are scattered maples, but as the SHT climbs, the maples dominate. Trail climbs steeply.

1.0 (6.6) First outcrop view

SHT comes to first view of valley. Trail continues up rocky ridgeline. Note occasional oak trees, a sign of drier microclimates on ridgelines. In late fall, look for Lake Superior views. A little further up, follow short spur to another dramatic view. The widest view comes at open rocky ridge, a common rock-climbing area known as "Section 13." Spectacular views from here of steep rock cliffs, inland ridges, beaver pond, and old Finland radar base. SHT continues to another rock outcrop (again, with seasonal Lake Superior views), then descends into a cedar-filled gulch.

▲ Section 13 Campsite

Tent pads: 4
Water: No water source—get water 0.5 miles south of campsite at Sawmill Creek or 0.5 miles north of campsite from small creek/beaver pond
Setting: In woods on top of Section 13 cliffs
Previous campsite: 5.8 miles
Next campsite: 3.8 miles

1.8 (5.8) Spur to overlook

This unmaintained 0.8-mile spur loop climbs to views of cliffs, then comes to another set of views from rocky, red pine ridge, before looping back. Main SHT descends through cedars along unnamed creek, then crosses beaver pond. Watch footing on descent. Section 13 cliffs tower above the trees. Trail travels through mixed forest over low-lying areas with short boardwalks and then continues to large beaver pond called Sawmill Pond.

3.0 (4.6) Boardwalk at Sawmill Pond

SHT crosses 440 feet of boardwalk over beaver dam. There is a bench on the west side, good for a lunch spot. Trail ascends through previously-logged area. Look south here for a great view of the Section 13 cliffs. SHT continues through open area, then enters mixed forest and passes by huge rock, called a glacial erratic. Trail enters logged areas so watch out for cross trails. Lots of wildflowers blooming in

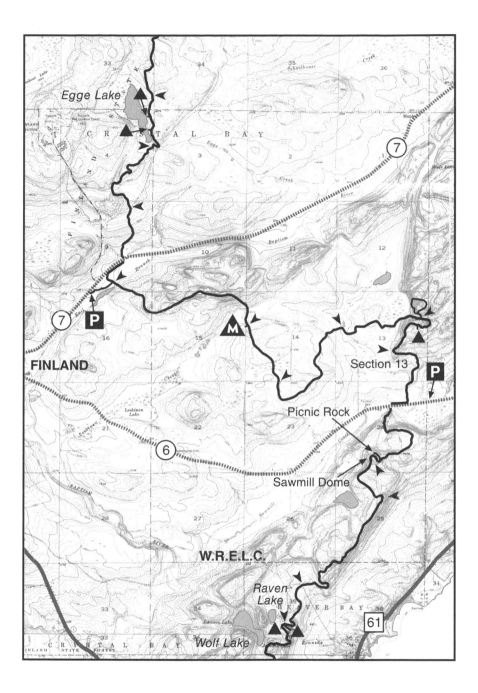

Egge Lake

CRYSTAL BAY

FINLAND

⑦

P

⑥

M

Section 13

P

Picnic Rock

Sawmill Dome

W.R.E.L.C.

Raven
Lake

Wolf Lake

BEAVER BAY

61

Protecting Egge Lake

The next section of the SHT includes beautiful Egge Lake. The rolling landscape of Egge Lake is part of a 700-acre parcel that was privately owned until 1999. The Nature Conservancy of Minnesota had an option to buy it, but offered this option to the Parks and Trails Council of Minnesota. The Council is a non-profit group that, according to its mission statement, "acts to help establish, develop and enhance Minnesota's parks and trails, and to encourage their protection and enjoyment." The Council bought the land, to swap for land owned by Lake County but held within the boundary of Crosby Manitou State Park. The Egge Lake parcel is to become county forest, and the park's holdings will get bigger.

The end result is that this beautiful tract of northern hardwood forest will be preserved within a larger county forest management scheme. Left to private ownership, this inland lake could have been developed with roads and cabins. Collaboration between businesses, non-profit groups and government saved the day.

season. SHT leaves plantation area on northeast side and descends through mixed forest to Park Hill Road.

4.4 (3.2) Park Hill Road

No parking here. SHT enters bog area with long boardwalks. Look closely and you might see a lady slipper. SHT moves through deciduous forest, across old logging road and descends to Leskinen Campsite and Creek.

5.2 (2.4) Leskinen Creek Campsite

▲ Leskinen Creek Campsite

Tent pads: 8
Water: from Leskinen Creek, unreliable in dry conditions
Setting: In woods on creek
Previous campsite: 3.8 miles
Next campsite: 4.7 miles

SHT climbs gradually away from creek through mixed forest, then climbs more steeply to top of ridge. SHT descends from ridge, then up to second ridge with views to southeast toward Sawmill Dome and Lake Superior. SHT descends to Finland Ski Trail and follows it downhill. Watch for signs. SHT descends to East Branch of

Baptism River. Bridge here is shared with the ski trail. SHT goes north along Tower Creek for 0.1 miles to junction with spur trail to Finland Recreation Center parking lot.

7.3 (0.3) Junction with spur trail
SHT spur trail goes 0.3 miles southwest through mixed forest to Finland Recreation Center parking lot.

7.6 (0.0) Finland Recreation Center trailhead parking lot

Finland Recreation Center to Crosby-Manitou State Park

11.8 miles

Section description: Finland Recreation Center on Lake Co. Rd. 7 (Cramer Rd.) to Crosby-Manitou State Park on Co. Rd. 7

Access and parking: *Directions to beginning trailhead:* At Hwy. 61 milepost 59.3, turn left on Hwy. 1 and go 6.0 miles to Lake Co. Rd. 7 (Cramer Rd.). Turn right and go 1.3 miles to parking lot past ball field at Finland Recreation Center. Overnight parking okay.

There is another parking option for this section: There is an option to make this a 7.5 mile hike by parking at the SHT parking lot on Sonju Lake Road. *Directions:* At Hwy. 61 milepost 59.3, turn left on Hwy. 1 and go 6.0 miles to Lake Co. Rd. 7 (Cramer Rd.). Turn right and go 6.8 miles. Turn left on Sonju Lake Rd. and go 2.3 miles to parking lot on left.

Facilities at starting trailhead: outhouses at parking lot

Designated campsites on this section: seven

Synopsis: This section, while longer, is relatively level hiking. It offers a wide variety of terrain and forest types. SHT passes through beautiful maple forests, groves of large cedar, excellent moose habitat and two spectacular inland lakes. Unique features of this section are the old trapper's cabin and the boardwalk to the island on Sonju Lake.

Mile-by-Mile Description

0.0 (11.8) Parking lot

From parking lot, a 0.3-mile spur goes to main SHT. SHT turns left, reaches Co. Rd. 7, turns right and follows road for 0.2 miles. Trail turns left and enters hardwood forest dominated by maples. SHT crosses old logging road before coming to North Shore State Trail (snowmobile trail).

1.1 (10.7) North Shore State Trail

SHT crosses North Shore State Trail, route of the John Beargrease Sled Dog Marathon each winter, and continues through mixed forest of birch, balsam fir and cedar. Trail follows 200 feet of boardwalk, then continues gentle ascent. SHT crosses unnamed creek and climbs gently with forest becoming predominantly maple.

2.3 (9.5) Egge Lake

SHT reaches Egge Lake, then follows Egge Creek steeply downhill. SHT crosses creek over scenic gorge, then doubles back toward Egge Lake. Trail continues along ridge above Egge Lake. After South and North Egge Lake campsites, trail passes under tree that forms a natural arch and continues through maple forest.

▲ South Egge Lake Campsite

Tent pads: 4
Water: From Egge Lake
Setting: On lake shore
Previous campsite: 4.7 miles
Next campsite: 0.2 miles

▲ North Egge Lake Campsite

Tent pads: 4
Water: From Egge Lake
Setting: On lake shore
Previous campsite: 0.2 miles
Next campsite: 3.1 miles

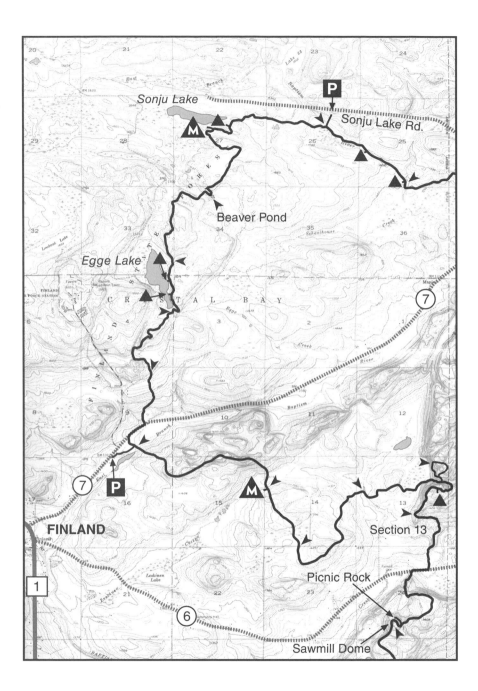

Sonju Lake

Sonju Lake

P

Sonju Lake Rd.

M

Beaver Pond

Egge Lake

C R Y S T A L   B A Y

7

7

P

FINLAND

M

Section 13

1

6

Picnic Rock

Sawmill Dome

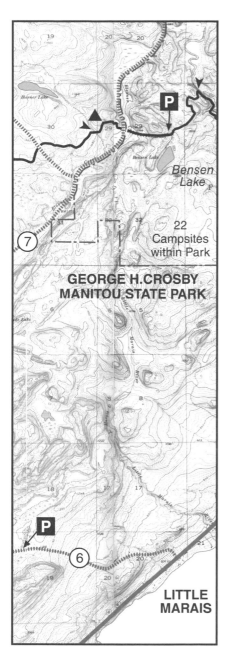

3.0 (8.8) Old trapper's cabin

SHT passes by deteriorated trapper's cabin. After leaving cabin, SHT enters cedar grove. Observe numbers on trees; this was most likely study site in past. SHT passes a natural rock ledge bench, then turns and climbs away from Egge Lake, descends into ravine, then climbs again.

4.4 (7.4) Beaver pond

SHT crosses boardwalk over beaver pond and follows around pond. Beaver lodge is visible at turn in trail. Trail ascends from beaver pond through alternating cedar and maple forests.

5.9 (5.9) South Sonju Lake Campsite

SHT turns onto a ridge that overlooks Sonju Lake, then descends to lake shore. After the South Sonju Lake Campsite, a spur trail with 80-foot boardwalk leads to a small island, named Lily Island after a dog who loved the trail, with a view of lake. Watch for moose feeding in lake.

⛺ South Sonju Lake Campsite

Tent pads: 6
Water: From Sonju Lake
Setting: 200 feet from lake shore
Previous campsite: 3.1 miles
Next campsite: 0.3 miles

▲ North Sonju Lake Campsite

Tent pads: 4
Water: From Sonju Lake—dock allows easy access to water
Setting: On lake shore
Previous campsite: 0.3 miles
Next campsite: 1.9 miles

6.2 (5.6) Sonju Creek

After crossing Sonju Creek, SHT leaves cedar grove and enters logged area with immature spruce and planted red pine, then descends to 80-foot boardwalk, enters cedar forest, then comes to open, rocky area with valley below. The valley is prime moose habitat. Trail then crosses logging road into spruce plantation.

7.5 (4.3) East Branch Baptism River crossing

SHT crosses river on bridge and continues downstream. To left is spur trail to parking lot on Sonju Lake Rd. SHT continues along river bank.

▲ East Branch Baptism River Campsite

Tent pads: 4
Water: From river
Setting: On river bank
Previous campsite: 1.9 miles
Next campsite: 0.6 miles

8.7 (3.1) Blesner Creek Campsite

▲ Blesner Creek Campsite

Tent pads: 3
Water: From river or creek
Setting: In cedar grove at intersection of creek and river
Previous campsite: 0.6 miles
Next campsite: 2.1 miles

SHT crosses Blesner Creek which flows from Blesner Lake, named for an early 20th century homesteader. SHT crosses North Shore State Trail again next to bridge across river and soon heads away from river through mixed forest including large cedar grove before crossing Sonju Lake Rd.

10.6 (1.2) Blesner Lake Rd.

SHT crosses Blesner Lake Rd. and comes to Aspen Knob campsite.

▲ Aspen Knob Campsite

Tent pads: 2
Water: From unnamed creek 300 feet away on SHT, unreliable in dry conditions
Setting: On a knob in woods
Previous campsite: 2.1 miles
Next campsite: 5.1 miles (or use Crosby-Manitou State Park campsites)

After campsite, trail climbs to knoll overlooking Baptism River valley before descending to Co. Rd. 7. Trail crosses road and follows entrance road 0.9 miles to Crosby-Manitou State Park.

11.8 (0.0) Crosby-Manitou State Park parking lot

Crosby-Manitou State Park to Caribou River Wayside
8.0 miles

Section description: Crosby-Manitou State Park on Lake Co. Rd. 7 (Cramer Rd.) to Caribou River Wayside

Access and parking: *Directions to beginning trailhead:* At Hwy. 61 milepost 59.3, turn left on Hwy. 1 and go 6.0 miles to Lake Co. Rd. 7 (Cramer Rd.). Turn right and go 7.8 miles to entrance of Crosby-Manitou State Park. Turn right and go 0.9 miles to trailhead parking lot. State park sticker required. Overnight parking okay.

Facilities at starting trailhead: outhouse

Designated campsites on this section: two (There are 22 fee campsites in Crosby-Manitou State Park—sites 3 and 4 in park are on SHT. Note: the self-registration board is on the west side of the park. If you're hiking from the east and want to camp in the park, you either have to hike to this board or make a reservation in advance).

Synopsis: This section of the SHT is quite dramatic in terms of topography, offering broad views of both inland ridges, ponds, and rivers, and of Lake Superior. The SHT here is more rugged than most sections and visits a variety of forest habitats. The western half of the section skirts the valley of the wild Manitou River, while the eastern half explores the cedar groves of the Little Manitou drainage and the dramatic Caribou River gorge.

Mile-by-Mile Description

0.0 (8.0) Parking lot
SHT leaves from parking lot at map board by outhouse on "Middle Trail," travels through birch forest, past large glacial erratic and across plank bridges. Spur trail on right side leads 70 yards to view of Lake Superior and Manitou River valley. SHT descends steeply through cedars.

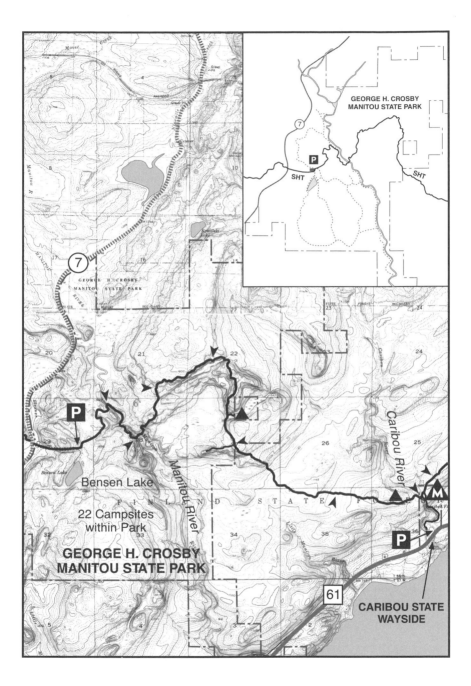

GEORGE H. CROSBY
MANITOU STATE PARK

Caribou River

P

GEORGE H. CROSBY
MANITOU STATE PARK

Bensen Lake

22 Campsites
within Park

GEORGE H. CROSBY
MANITOU STATE PARK

Manitou River

M

P

61

CARIBOU STATE
WAYSIDE

George H. Crosby-Manitou State Park

George H. Crosby-Manitou State Park is known for its rugged beauty and fine fishing. The wild and scenic Manitou River runs through the park on its descent to Lake Superior. George Crosby, an early mining magnate, donated the property for use as a state park with the provision that development be limited. With his wishes in mind, the first backpack-only park was designed. Today visitors camp at one of many remote backpack sites located mainly along the river. Hikers self-register for sites at the camping registration board. There are 23 miles of trails in this 6,682 acre park, and fishing—especially for trout along the river or on Benson Lake—is among the most popular park uses. Because of the relatively undisturbed nature of the park it is common to encounter a variety of wildlife, such as deer and moose, or less frequently, timber wolf, vole, mink, and pileated woodpecker.

0.9 (7.1) Junction of SHT/Middle Trail with River Trail

Upriver from this junction about 0.25 miles are the Manitou Cascades, a worthy side trip. At junction, SHT goes downriver (right), past state park campsites 3 and 4, and up and over two bluffs with partial overlooks of river valley. Signpost marks where SHT goes steeply downhill to Manitou River bridge, descending through dark spruce forest and overlook 100 yards before river and bridge. Overlook allows glimpses through forest of tumbling river as it descends toward bridge.

1.6 (6.4) Bridge over Manitou River

The Manitou River is one of the most rugged river valleys along North Shore. SHT crosses river, travels past white pine on east side of valley, then into scrubby mixed woods of fir, birch, and aspen. Steep climb is 600 yards long and 300 feet up. SHT passes series of four overlooks with views of Lake Superior and Manitou River valley.

2.3 (5.7) View of pond

After climbing short rocky slope, there is a pond view with birch/balsam hill behind it. Look for variety of lichens growing on rock. Next overlook includes Lake Superior and old Air Force radar base near

Finland (white buildings). SHT continues along hilltop, alternating between maple woods and stunning views of Lake Superior. Note juneberry trees and sumac at rocky openings. Beaver ponds are visible below. SHT eventually descends again into deep fault line valley.

3.4 (4.6) Stream crossing small beaver dam

SHT climbs away from stream through balsam, birch, and cedar. Forest changes over to maple, then birch and spruce. Trail comes to series of overlooks of Little Manitou River and spectacular maple hillsides. This area is known as "Horseshoe Ridge." Rock underfoot changes to crumbly lava gravel. Trail passes cedar and white pine.

4.5 (3.5) Horsehoe Ridge Campsite

▲ Horseshoe Ridge Campsite

Tent pads: 4
Water: From small creek just east of campsite, unreliable in dry conditions
Setting: Nestled in woods below Horseshoe Ridge
Previous campsite: 5.1 miles (or use Crosby-Manitou State Park campsites)
Next campsite: 3.1 miles

Bridges on the Superior Hiking Trail

Some of the trail's most remarkable construction involves bridgework. Each stream that crosses the SHT is bridged, so hikers don't have to get wet or ford rivers. Over 100 bridges of various lengths, materials, and construction link embankments and landscapes. A volunteer crew can make small wooden walkways, but some bridges are elaborately designed and need the transport of considerable lumber and other materials. The Baptism River suspension bridge, for example, required helicopter transport of supplies because of its complexity and location. The DNR State Parks Division, using Lake Superior Coastal Program grants, built four new bridges on the Manitou, Caribou, Cross, and Kadunce rivers from 2007-2010.

After campsite, SHT continues on a long rocky ridge featuring oak trees. After descending, trail continues through cedar swamp with plank walkways.

6.2 (1.8) Logging road

After crossing road built by Bob Silver for selectively cutting cedar in this area, SHT moves into birch/balsam woods, then a small rock outcrop and through spruces and bracken ferns. Between logging road and Caribou River, SHT crosses historic Pork Bay Trail, a Native American and voyageur trail that led from Pork Bay nine miles inland to Nine-Mile Lake. Listen for Caribou River as SHT descends.

▲ West Caribou River campsite

Tent pads: 2
Water: From Caribou River
Setting: On hill above Caribou River 0.3 miles from bridge
Previous campsite: 3.1 miles
Next campsite: 0.3 miles

7.3 (0.7) Bridge over Caribou River

After crossing bridge, main SHT continues upstream (left). 0.7 mile spur trail goes downstream to Hwy. 61 parking lot. After 0.1 miles, spur trail on right goes on stair structure to base of Caribou Falls.

8.0 (0.0) Caribou River Wayside (Hwy. 61)

Caribou River Wayside to Cook County Road 1
9.0 miles

Section description: Caribou River Wayside on Hwy. 61 to Cook Co. Rd. 1 (Cramer Rd.)

Access and parking: *Directions to beginning trailhead:* At Hwy. 61 milepost 70.5 on left side of highway. Overnight parking is not allowed.

There is another parking option for this section: There is an additional parking lot on Sugarloaf Road affording shorter day hikes of 3.5 miles or 5.5 miles. At Hwy. 61 milepost 73.3 turn north and go 1.5 miles to parking lot on left.

Facilities at starting trailhead: none

Designated campsites on this section: four

Synopsis: After ascending the beautiful and dramatic Caribou River gorge, this section of the SHT follows a series of ridges and overlooks through mixed forest, including one of the most beautiful pure birch stands on the trail. The bog vegetation of the Alfred's Pond area is a quiet highlight. Although this section is lengthy, it is one of the easier sections to hike—perfect for a long nature walk, with an abundance of wildflowers, including the pink ladyslipper in June. There is one long steep descent just before Dyer's Creek.

Mile-by-Mile Description

0.0 (9.0) Parking lot off Hwy. 61
Spur trail leaves from north end of parking lot. There is another short spur off from this spur that goes to base of Caribou Falls at 0.6 miles.

Main spur continues along gorge of Caribou River through pine and spruce to junction with main trail.

0.7 (8.3) Junction with main SHT

After passing bridge on Caribou River and campsite, main SHT follows small stream, then travels through past logging area.

⛺ East Caribou River Campsite

Tent pads: 10
Water: From Caribou River
Setting: On hill above Caribou River, close to bridge
Previous campsite: 0.3 mile
Next campsite: 1.2 miles

1.2 (7.8) Logging road

After logging road, SHT follows ridge on old logging road and then crosses powerline and goes through mixed hardwoods and beautiful birch forest, with seasonal view of Lake Superior.

2.0 (7.0) Spur to campsite

Right after campsite spur trail, SHT crosses Crystal Creek on covered bridge, then continues through marvelous birch forest. If you want, follow Crystal Creek down to collapsed mine shaft. At this mine, note wide band of calcite crystals in bottom of creek's gorge. These crystals led a prospector to believe there would be ore there also.

▲ Crystal Creek Campsite

Tent pads: 4
Water: From Crystal Creek, unreliable in dry conditions
Setting: On spur trail 200 yards off SHT in birch forest
Previous campsite: 1.2 miles
Next campsite: 2.4 miles

After campsite, SHT passes through large birch forest, crosses powerline and private road and passes through red pine plantations.

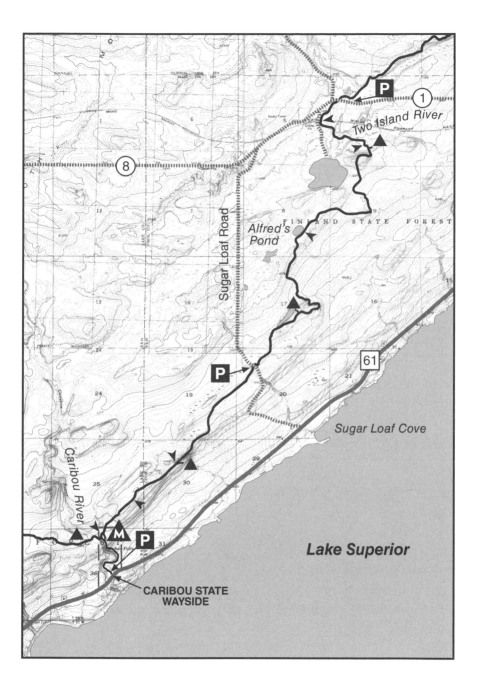

Two Island River

8

Sugar Loaf Road

Alfred's
Pond

FINLAND STATE FOREST

P

61

P

Sugar Loaf Cove

Caribou River

M P

Lake Superior

CARIBOU STATE
WAYSIDE

Bogs on the Trail

Bogs are a type of wetland common in northern Minnesota, though less common along the Superior Hiking Trail. Bogs are characterized by a lush growth of sphagnum moss and high acidity. Since the bog is a nutrient-poor environment, some bog plants have evolved insect eating as a way of getting needed nutrients like nitrogen. The pitcher plant and sundew are two insectivorous plants common in the bogs in northern Minnesota. The sundew is a tiny plant usually found on the edge of the mat close to water. It has sticky tipped hairs on its leaves that trap insects. The pitcher plant is much bigger, perhaps a foot across, and traps insects in its hollow, fluid-filled leaves. Bogs are fascinating places to explore, but please use the boardwalk provided.

3.5 (5.5) Sugar Loaf Rd.

After parking lot, SHT crosses Sugar Loaf Rd., crosses a stream on a bridge with spindle post railings, then travels through mixed forest and by Sugarloaf Pond, an old beaver pond.

4.5 (4.5) Sugarloaf Pond Campsite

▲ Sugarloaf Pond Campsite

Tent pads: 4
Water: pond
Setting: On beaver pond; pond is drying up so this is a difficult water source. You may have to travel through mud to get to water.
Previous campsite: 2.4 miles
Next campsite: 3.5 miles

SHT continues through sometimes wet soil and crosses several logging roads before Alfred's Pond.

5.8 (3.2) Alfred's Pond

Look for bog plants like carnivorous pitcher plant and sundew, as well as sphagnum moss, orchids, and blue-flag iris. A floating walkway allows one to see everything without getting wet or damaging the bog. After pond, SHT travels through wet area, mostly on boardwalk. Trail climbs uphill, with nice views, then descends steep downhill into birch valley.

7.9 (1.1) Dyer's Creek Campsite

▲ Dyer's Creek Campsite

Tent pads: 4
Water: From Dyer's Creek
Setting: Near confluence of Two Island River and Dyer's
 Creek in birch forest
Previous campsite: 3.5 miles
Next campsite: 2.9 miles

After crossing Dyer's Creek on a bridge, SHT continues upstream along Two Island River, then ascends through mixed conifers.

8.6 (0.4) Dyer's Lake Rd. crossing

SHT comes to Dyer's Lake Rd., turns right and travels on road across railroad tracks. SHT leaves Dyer's Lake Rd. and goes back into woods on right. Trail crosses Cook Co. Rd. 1 (Cramer Rd.) and comes to trailhead parking lot.

9.0 (0.0) Cook Co. Rd. 1 (Cramer Rd.) parking lot

Cook County Road 1 to Temperance River State Park

8.0 miles

Section description: Cook Co. Rd. 1 (Cramer Rd.) to Temperance River Wayside on Hwy. 61

Access and parking: *Directions to beginning trailhead:* At Hwy. 61 milepost 78.8, turn left on Cook Co. Rd. 1 (Cramer Rd.) and go 3.6 miles to parking lot on right. Overnight parking okay.

Facilities at starting trailhead: none

Designated campsites on this section: five

Synopsis: The climb to Tower Overlook through a rich old growth maple forest, the descent to Fredenberg Creek, and the hike along the marsh named Boney's Meadow, with a chance to see moose, set the stage for the highlight of the section, the historic Cross and Temperance Rivers.

There are two additional parking options for this section:

1) SHT trailhead parking lot on Skou Rd. At Hwy. 61 milepost 78.1, turn left and go 0.1 mile to small parking lot on right at 90-degree turn in road. A 1.5 mile-spur trail goes to the main trail. Spur trail starts by sharing ski trail, then eventually leaves ski trail and follows along Cross River high above river. Nice bench and view of the Cross River where the spur trail meets the main trail. The section total is 6.8 miles. Overnight parking okay.

2) SHT trailhead parking lot on Forest Rd. 343 (Temperance River Rd.). At Hwy. 61 milepost 80.2, turn left (north) and go 0.9 miles to trailhead parking lot on left. The section total is 7.2 miles. Overnight parking okay.

Mile-by-Mile Description

0.0 (8.0) Parking lot

SHT passes through mixed conifer area, then ascends into Superior National Forest Northern Hardwood Research Natural Area. This is one of richest maple forests along trail. Wildflower viewing along this section of trail in spring is fantastic. SHT climbs to Tower Overlook, with beautiful view of Lake Superior, then descends.

1.8 (6.2) Fredenberg Creek

100 feet after footbridge, there is a short spur trail to campsite. SHT follows creek, then follows edge of marsh, known locally as Boney's Meadow. Look for moose tracks near marsh.

▲ Fredenberg Creek Campsite

Tent pads: 5
Water: From Fredenberg Creek
Setting: In maple forest
Previous campsite: 2.9 miles
Next campsite: 2.0 miles

2.9 (5.1) Gasco Rd.

SHT crosses historic logging road. Trail enters spruce plantation, then hardwood forest, then descends to a lowland. Trail reaches bluff of Cross River.

3.8 (4.2) Falls on Cross River

SHT comes to great view of falls, and over a mile of trail along the Cross River. Trail follows edge of river up and down steep bluffs. Look for beaver activity on side streams.

▲ Falls Campsite

Tent pads: 3
Water: From Cross River
Setting: Uphill from Cross River
Previous campsite: 2.0 miles
Next campsite: 0.8 miles

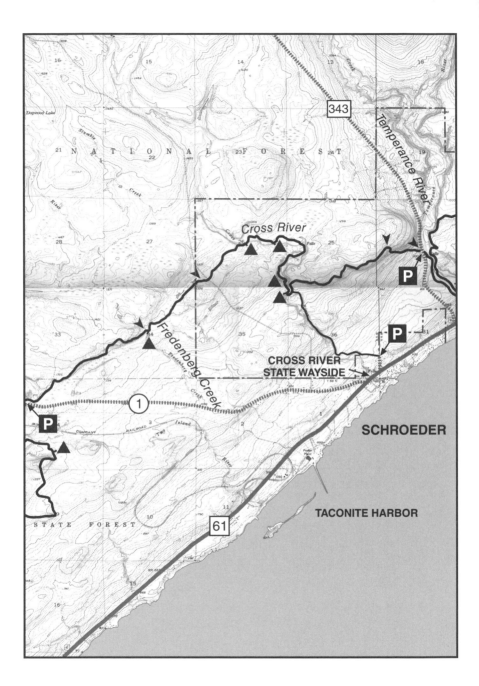

CROSS RIVER
STATE WAYSIDE

SCHROEDER

TACONITE HARBOR

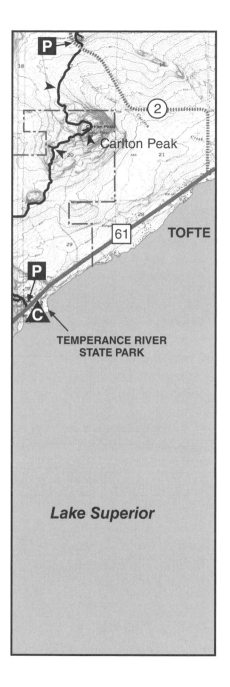

Temperance River State Park

The Temperance River was presumably so named because, unlike other North Shore streams, this river had no bar at its mouth. The 500-acre park is best known for its deep, narrow river gorge, waterfalls, and the glacial potholes that dot the river valley. Fishing is popular on the Temperance and nearby Cross Rivers, where several species of trout and salmon have been stocked and have become established. Two campgrounds with a total of 50 sites are popular because of their lakeside location. Eight miles of trails connect with the North Shore State Trail, the SHT and Superior National Forest trails, and provide recreational use year around. Picnic sites are located along Lake Superior adjacent to the lower campground.

Gitchi Gami State Trail

When completed over the next decade, the Gitchi-Gami State Trail (GGST) will be an 86-mile non-motorized, paved trail between Two Harbors and Grand Marais for bicyclists, in-line skaters, joggers, and walkers. Much like the Superior Hiking Trail, the Gitchi-Gami Trail will connect communities, state parks and attractions along the North Shore of Lake Superior. More information about the trail can be found at www.GGTA.org. It is possible at some locations to hike on the Superior Hiking Trail and bike back to the starting point on the GGST. The longest completed segment is from Gooseberry Falls State Park to Beaver Bay. The SHT crosses the GGST at Temperance River State Park.

▲ Ledge Campsite

Tent pads: 2
Water: From Cross River
Setting: Uphill from
    Cross River
Previous campsite:
    0.8 miles
Next campsite: 0.8 miles

5.3 (2.7) Cross River campsites and bridge

▲ North Cross River Campsite

Tent pads: 2
Water: From Cross River
Setting: On Cross River
Previous campsite:
    0.8 miles
Next campsite: 0.1 miles

▲ South Cross River Campsite

Tent pads: 4
Water: From Cross River
Setting: on Cross River
Previous campsite: 0.1 miles
Next campsite: 9.1 miles (or
    use Temperance River
    State Park)

After campsites, SHT crosses bridge over river. At the trail junction after bridge, main SHT goes upstream and 1.5 mile spur trail on right goes to Skou Rd. in Schroeder. Main SHT follows bluff, then travels along ridgeline, with views of Lake Superior and Taconite Harbor.

6.4 (1.6) Top of ridge
After ridge, SHT descends steeply through birch-aspen forest. Watch your footing here on crumbly soil.

7.2 (0.8) Temperance River Rd. (Forest Rd. 343)
SHT crosses road and heads downstream along river as Temperance River changes from wide, quiet river to roaring cascade in narrow gorges. SHT joins state park ski trail for about 0.3 miles, then turns sharply left to follow edge of gorge for about 200 yards before reaching metal bridge. After crossing bridge, spur trail goes downstream 0.2 miles to parking lot. Main SHT goes upstream to Carlton Peak and beyond.

8.0 (0.0) Temperance River Wayside parking lot
On Hwy. 61.

History of the Cross River

Hugging the banks of this spirited river for over a mile, the SHT gives ample opportunity to observe the various antics of the rushing water—site of any number of interesting historical events. The Voyageurs portaged this stretch of rapids to reach the calm headwaters, a chain of inland lakes, and eventually Lake Vermilion, near Tower. By the turn of the century, loggers had entered the watershed and used the river for the roaring spring log drive down to the boom at the mouth. This included putting a series of dams on the river. The logging business ceased operations in 1905 due in part to a smallpox epidemic.

Temperance River State Park to Britton Peak

4.8 miles

Section description: Temperance River Wayside on Hwy. 61 to Britton Peak parking lot on Cook Co. Rd. 2 (Sawbill Trail)

Access and parking: *Directions to beginning trailhead:* At Hwy. 61 milepost 80.3 on left side of highway. Look for SHT sign. Overnight parking at wayside is not allowed. For overnight parking, check in at state park office to be directed to parking area. State park sticker required for overnight parking.

Facilities at starting trailhead: none.

Designated campsites on this section: none

Synopsis: This is one of the most easily accessible sections of the SHT and one of the most hiked. The hike to Carlton Peak from either direction climbs steeply, and the short but steep scramble to the top of the peak has ample rewards of incredible views. Coming from Temperance River State Park, the hiker also gets to see the amazing Temperance River, roaring deep in a dark basaltic canyon.

Mile-by-Mile Description

0.0 (4.8) Trailhead at Temperance River Wayside parking lot
Spur trail on east side of river joins main SHT at bridge at 0.2 miles and continues upstream. Trail joins ski trail at switchback and climbs high on rim over river.

1.2 (3.6) SHT leaves river
After leaving river, SHT enters scrubby woods, then aspen forest. Trail shares ski trail. Look for signs of old white pines and fire. Two major fires have swept through here. Trail turns steeply uphill, leaving ski trail and climbing through birches.

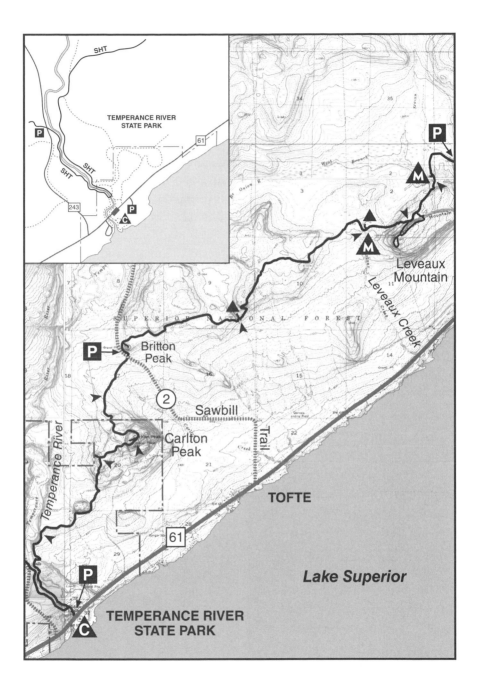

Carlton Peak

The high points on the North Shore landscape exist because they are made of rocks that have been more resistant to weathering and erosion over the billion years since they were formed. Carlton Peak is a prime example, made of several huge blocks of whitish anorthosite rock. These blocks were carried or floated up from the base of the earth's crust, 25 or 30 miles below, suspended in molten diabase magma. With very few natural fractures, these anorthosite blocks or "inclusions" also make up many of the knobs and hills in and around Silver Bay and Tettegouche State Park. A climb to the top of Carlton Peak reveals some tremendous views, which is why this was the site of a fire tower up until the 1950s (the foundation is all that is left of the tower). Ted Tofte Overlook is above anorthosite quarry.

2.6 (2.2) Overlook spur

Look for sign and follow spur 80 yards for a view of Lake Superior, Temperance River valley, and Taconite Harbor. Main SHT continues through pure birch forest, past a spur with an old access road and ski trail to Carlton Peak. SHT begins gradual ascent counterclockwise around Carlton Peak, through large fallen boulders. This is a popular rock climbing site and the only difficult hiking on this section.

3.4 (1.4) Spur trail to summit

SHT reaches trail register and continues 15 feet past register to spur trail to top of Carlton Peak on left. After summit, main SHT continues through woods reaching spur trail to Ted Tofte Overlook on right. Trail travels by high rock walls and then gradually descends with occasional views.

4.0 (0.8) Ski trail

SHT travels through maple forest, then a spruce plantation with lots of wooden walkways to cross muddy areas. Trail reenters woods, crosses ski trail, then crosses Sawbill Trail and winds into Britton Peak parking lot.

4.8 (0.0) Britton Peak parking lot

Britton Peak to Oberg Mountain

5.7 miles

Section description: Britton Peak parking lot on Cook Co. Rd. 2 (Sawbill Trail) to Oberg Mountain parking lot on Forest Rd. 336 (Onion River Rd.)

Access and parking: *Directions to beginning trailhead:* At Hwy. 61 milepost 82.8, turn left on Cook Co. Rd. 2 (Sawbill Trail) and go 2.7 miles to parking lot on right. Overnight parking okay.

Facilities at starting trailhead: outhouse

Designated campsites on this section: four

Synopsis: The section, one of the easier of the SHT, begins as an easy, rolling path through maple and birch forest. Right at the start of the section, there is a very steep 0.2 mile spur trail to Britton Peak with great views. The topography becomes more dramatic in the central section and the maple and birch give way to spruce, balsam, and cedar around the beaver pond. From the pond the trail ascends to the Leveaux Mountain loop and on to the parking area. Wet and seasonally wet ground is typical along this section.

Mile-by-Mile Description

0.0 (5.7) Parking area
Right after SHT leaves parking lot, spur on right goes steeply up 0.2 miles to overlook near top of Britton Peak. View from top is dominated by Carlton Peak in distance. There is a memorial for W.L. Britton, a WWII veteran who worked for Forest Service for two years. His ashes were strewn on Britton Peak in 1947. Main SHT continues through dense sugar maple forest. SHT crosses ski trails frequently, at 0.2, 1.2, and 1.4 miles.

1.6 (4.1) Wooden bridge at Springdale Creek

After crossing bridge, SHT passes campsite and ski trail, then climbs through young sugar maple stand to overlook with view of Lake Superior and Apostle Islands 30 miles away.

▲ Springdale Creek Campsite

Tent pads: 4
Water: From creek, unreliable during dry conditions
Setting: On hill above creek
Previous campsite: 9.1 miles (or use Temperance River State Park)
Next campsite: 2.5 miles

4.2 (1.5) Bridge across Leveaux beaver pond

After crossing bridge, look for beaver lodge to north and watch for moose. SHT campsite is 0.2 miles past bridge. SHT crosses ski trail, enters cedar grove, then enters maple forest beneath the cliffs of Leveaux Mountain.

▲ West Leveaux Pond Campsite

Tent pads: 8
Water: From beaver pond
Setting: Near beaver pond
Previous campsite: 2.5 miles
Next campsite: 0.1 miles

▲ East Leveaux Pond Campsite

Tent pads: 4
Water: From beaver pond
Setting: Near beaver pond.
Previous campsite: 0.1 miles
Next campsite: 1.2 miles

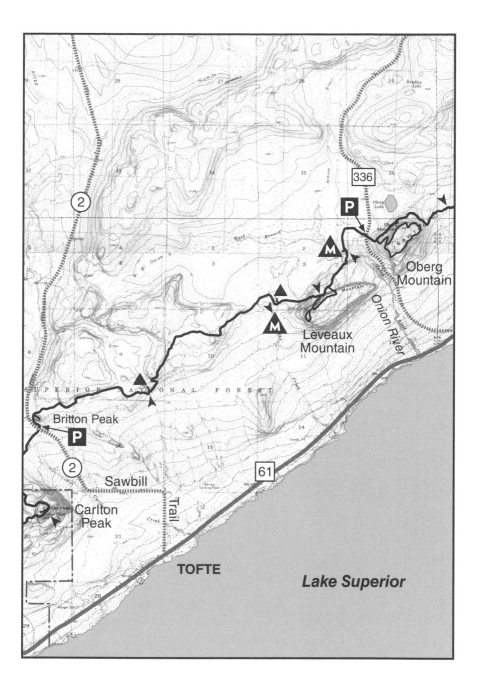

Lake Superior

TOFTE

Britton Peak

Carlton
Peak

Sawbill

Leveaux
Mountain

Oberg
Mountain

Onion River

SUPERIOR NATIONAL FOREST

4.5 (1.2) West junction of Leveaux Mountain spur trail loop

1.3 mile spur trail loop goes to top of Leveaux Mountain for several grand Lake Superior overlooks. West end of spur trail is less steep than east end. On main SHT, trail comes to east junction 0.2 miles after west junction.

5.1 (0.6) Bridge at Onion River

Campsite is in spruce forest 0.1 miles past river.

⛺ Onion River Campsite

Tent pads: 8
Water: From Onion River
Setting: In woods above
   Onion River
Previous campsite: 1.2 miles
Next campsite: 2.0 miles

5.7 (0.0) Oberg Mountain trailhead parking lot

Oberg Mountain to Lutsen Mountains Recreation Area
7.0 miles

Section description: Oberg Mountain parking lot on Forest Rd. 336 (Onion River Rd.) to Lutsen Mountains Recreation Area, on Cook Co. Rd. 5 (Ski Hill Rd.)

Access and parking: *Directions to beginning trailhead:* At Hwy. 61 milepost 87.5, turn left on Forest Rd. 336 (Onion River Rd.) and go 2.2 miles to parking lot on left side of road. Overnight parking okay.

Facilities at starting trailhead: outhouse

Designated campsites on this section: three

Synopsis: This section has a bit of everything, from the scenic over-looks of Oberg Mountain and Moose Mountain to the dense maple forests of the northeastern end. After the optional 1.8 mile spur loop to Oberg Mountain, the main SHT winds through boreal forests of birch, spruce, balsam fir, and alder. The trail then climbs steeply to the top of Moose Mountain, where the views in all directions are rewarding, only to descend and climb and descend Mystery Mountain. The ups and downs make this a challenging section. The last three miles go through a rich maple forest before emerging at the gorge of the Poplar River. This section was constructed by the Forest Service and is one of the oldest sections of the SHT.

Mile-by-Mile Description

0.0 (7.0) Oberg Mountain parking lot

SHT leaves from east side of parking lot, up some wooden steps. Junction of Oberg Mountain loop at 0.2 miles, a great side trip of about 1.8 miles (see sidebar). Main SHT continues northeast around the base of Oberg Mountain through dense shrubs. Oberg Lake is visible through trees to

Oberg Loop

This is a 1.8-mile loop around the summit of Oberg Mountain. Oberg is covered by a rich maple forest, which gives out only at the many scenic overlooks. Work your way counterclockwise around the summit for about eight different overlooks in all directions, starting with Leveaux Mountain and Lake Superior (and a distant Carlton Peak), then Moose Mountain, and finally inland to Oberg Lake and the rolling crests of inland ridges. Trail is well-maintained and overlooks are developed for safety. This is a great hike any time of year, but especially in the fall when the colors of this mountain and Leveaux Mountain are at their peak.

north. SHT descends into wet area, then crosses Oberg Creek.

1.2 (5.8) Junction with ski trail

SHT crosses ski trail and also snowmobile trail and enters mixed forest, with tall aspen, a huge cedar tree, and lots of bluebead lily. Just before Rollins Creek is short spur to campsite.

▲ West Rollins Creek campsite

Tent pads: 5
Water: From Rollins Creek
Setting: In a large cedar grove on creek
Previous campsite: 2.0 miles
Next campsite: 0.1 miles

1.6 (5.4) Bridge over Rollins Creek

SHT follows creek upstream a ways, then ascends from valley up flank of Moose Mountain, through yellow birch, cedar, and spruce, then paper birch, aspen, and fir. SHT climbs steeply to top of ridge. Look for northern plants like shinleaf pyrola and twinflower near switchbacks on south side of Moose Mountain.

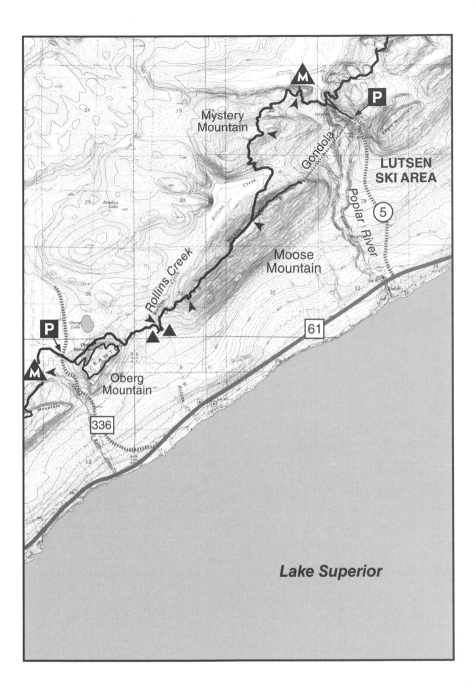

Mystery
Mountain

LUTSEN
SKI AREA

Gondola

Poplar River

Rollins Creek

Moose
Mountain

61

P

M

Oberg
Mountain

336

Lake Superior

▲ East Rollins Creek Campsite

Tent pads: 3
Water: From Rollins Creek
Setting: In woods on creek
Previous campsite: 0.1 mile
Next campsite: 4.5 miles

2.2 (4.8) Southwest end of Moose Mountain ridgetop

Moose Mountain is 1,688 feet above sea level and 1,086 feet above Lake Superior. SHT winds along ridgetop, with occasional views on both sides. Forest here is spruce, birch, and balsam fir. Listen for chatter of red squirrels.

3.4 (3.6) Spur to gondola

This 0.8 mile spur goes along the north side of Moose Mountain to top of gondola. A fun day hike is to take the gondola to the top of Moose Mountain and then hike back to the chalet, a total of 3.5 miles. Main SHT descends along north side of Moose Mountain. Descent is steep and rugged, with large basaltic outcroppings and a dark, shaded forest. SHT continues north across plank bridge (headwaters of Rollins Creek, which SHT crosses 1.5 miles to the southwest), and enters maple forest. Note all ages of maple trees, from seedling to mature. Trail ascends steeply out of creek valley up Mystery Mountain.

5.2 (1.8) Overlook

Small, unmarked overlook of Lutsen ski hills, gondola, and down Poplar River valley to Lake Superior. SHT continues in maple forest, then forest changes to birch and spruce. 0.25 miles before campsite, there is a spur to overlook marked by sign with views of Poplar River valley.

6.1 (0.9) Mystery Mtn. Campsite

▲ Mystery Mountain Campsite

Tent pads: 6
Water: 0.5 miles away at Poplar River
Setting: In woods
Previous campsite: 4.5 miles
Next campsite: 2.1 miles

Just past campsite is 10-yard spur to overlook over Poplar River and a spruce swamp. SHT descends steeply into wet area with scrubby alders, birches, thimbleberries, and raspberries. Trail turns left (downhill) onto Lutsen ski trail on old road (junction marked by SHT sign). SHT follows Poplar River gorge downstream on road, then crosses river on a wide bridge over a spectacular waterfall. Main SHT continues straight after bridge. Spur trail to parking lot turns right and follows road 0.1 miles to three-car SHT parking lot or continues an additional 0.3 miles to general parking areas at Lutsen Mountains recreation area. Watch signs carefully.

6.7 (0.3) SHT trailhead parking lot
SHT spur continues down dirt road to Chalet area.

7.0 (0.0) General parking at Lutsen Mountains

Ecology of North and South Slopes

Many factors lead to the particular kind of trees and other plants at any given point along the trail. One factor that is often apparent along the trail is the difference between north- and south-facing slopes. Experienced hikers know the old wisdom that moss grows on the north side of trees. The same holds true for the ridgelines of the North Shore. Along the ridgeline, the forest on the southern or Lake side receives significantly more sunshine than the forest on the northern, inland side. This added sunshine makes the forest warmer and drier, an environment friendly to trees of the northern hardwood type, such as birch, aspen, oak, and maple. The cooler, moister north-facing slopes have, in general, a more boreal feel, with spruces and fir, as well as the proverbial moss. Keep an eye out for these subtle changes.

Lutsen Mountains Recreation Area to Caribou Trail
6.4 miles

Section description: Lutsen Mountains Recreation Area, on Cook Co. Rd. 5 (Ski Hill Rd.) to Cook Co. Rd. 4 (Caribou Trail)

Access and parking: *Directions to beginning trailhead:* At Hwy. 61 mile-post 90.1, turn left on Cook Co. Rd. 5 (Ski Hill Rd.) and go 2.9 miles to recreation area. Park in general parking areas or continue 0.3 miles up road past gondola and restaurant to small trailhead parking lot on left. Overnight parking okay in both areas.

Facilities at starting trailhead: bathrooms, telephone, drinking water, restaurants, gift shop, lodging

Designated campsites on this section: four

Synopsis: This is a very scenic segment of the SHT, with a diverse forest ranging from a mature maple canopy to mixed birch, aspen, pine, and spruce. Stretches parallel the winding Poplar River and breathtaking Lake Agnes, and there are several open vistas of the Poplar River valley. In late summer it is a mushroom-hunter's heaven in terms of variety and supply.

Mile-by-Mile Description

0.0 (6.4) Trailhead parking lot

SHT spur trail follows gravel road uphill either from Lutsen Mountains general parking or from small SHT parking lot. Road splits uphill from small parking lot. Fork on right continues to main SHT. Once reaching main SHT, trail turns right off road and ascends sharply. SHT winds through switchbacks to overlook on ski area. Trail then enters mature maple forest and gently rolling terrain. SHT crosses ski/bike

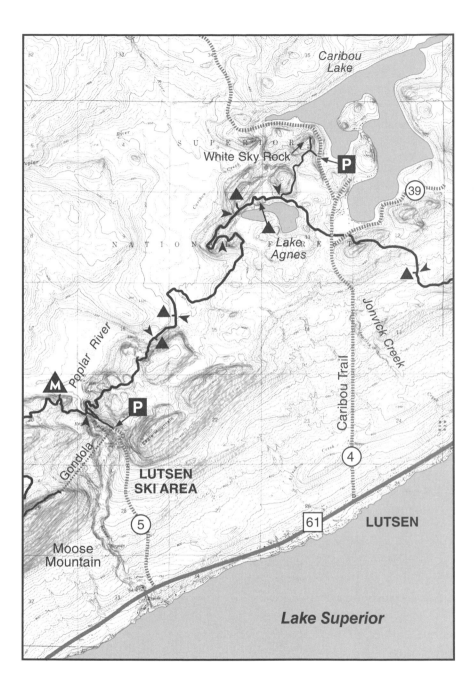

Caribou
Lake

White Sky Rock

P

39

Lake
Agnes

Johvick Creek

Poplar River

M

P

Caribou Trail

Gondola

LUTSEN
SKI AREA

4

5

61

LUTSEN

Moose
Mountain

Lake Superior

trail, then continues to Glove Overlook, a rock outcrop with views north and west of Poplar River valley. Trail winds down steeply through pine and aspen forest, coming to the Poplar River.

1.5 (4.9) West Poplar River Campsite

▲ West Poplar River Campsite

Tent pads: 3
Water: From Poplar River
Setting: On the river
Previous campsite: 2.1 miles
Next campsite: 0.6 miles

SHT follows river after campsite and crosses a snowmobile trail at 2.0 miles and stays on same side of river. This area is heavily travelled by moose, so keep an eye out for tracks, antler rubs, and possibly a glimpse of a moose.

2.1 (4.3) East Poplar River Campsite

▲ East Poplar River Campsite

Tent pads: 2
Water: From Poplar River
Setting: On the river
Previous campsite: 0.6 miles
Next campsite: 3.0 miles

SHT goes through spruce swamp with many footbridges. Trail leaves river and ascends into mature maple forest.

4.0 (2.4) Overlook on Poplar River
SHT comes to first of three outstanding overlooks of Poplar River valley. All three are good break spots, with views of Lake Superior and river far below

5.0 (1.4) Agnes Creek Bridge

After crossing bridge, SHT climbs steeply to dramatic Lake Agnes overlook by trail register. Trail descends to lakeshore and passes spur to campsite high above lake and campsite on lake. After campsites, the trail continues along the north side of Lake Agnes.

▲ West Lake Agnes Campsite

Tent pads: 4
Water: From Lake Agnes
Setting: In maple grove overlooking Lake Agnes
Previous campsite: 3.0 miles
Next campsite: 0.3 miles

▲ East Lake Agnes Campsite

Tent pads: 4
Water: From Lake Agnes
Setting: On lake shore
Previous campsite: 0.3 miles
Next campsite: 2.4 miles

5.6 (0.8) Spur trail to parking lot

Sign clearly marks directions and mileage. Main SHT continues along Lake Agnes and then continues through mixed forest to Co. Rd. 4 (Caribou Trail).

Spur trail turns left (north) from Lake Agnes and goes 0.8 miles to parking lot. It passes Cedar Hill, goes through a narrow rock canyon where a staircase has been sculpted from a single log and crosses a snowmobile trail. At junction in spur trail, a short 0.15 mile overlook spur trail goes left up to White Sky Rock with great view of Caribou Lake. Return to spur trail, which continues downhill, crosses Co. Rd. 4 and goes to parking lot.

6.4 (0.0) Caribou Trail trailhead parking lot

Caribou Trail to Cascade River State Park
11.0 miles

Section description: Cook Co. Rd. 4 (Caribou Trail) to Cascade River Wayside, on Hwy. 61

Access and parking: *Directions to beginning trailhead:* At Hwy. 61 milepost 92.0, turn left on Cook Co. Rd. 4 (Caribou Trail) and go 4.1 miles to Co. Rd. 94. Turn right and take immediate left to trailhead parking lot. Overnight parking okay.

Facilities at starting trailhead: outhouse

Designated campsites on this section: three

Synopsis: This section follows along ridgelines with many views of Lake Superior and inland ridges of the Sawtooth range. The variety of habitats is as broad as anywhere on the SHT, with everything from mature maple forests to dense groves of cedar, from a massive beaver pond to wide-open hillsides. It begins with a steep ascent but drops gently to a valley and crosses a beaver dam. It crosses several scenic creeks and travels through Cascade River State Park. Highlights include the views from White Sky Rock and Lookout Mountain and the waterfalls on the Cascade River.

Mile-by-Mile Description

0.0 (11.0) Caribou Trail parking lot
From the parking lot, spur trail crosses Caribou Trail and goes 0.8 miles to reach main SHT by Lake Agnes. There is an optional 0.15 mile spur trail to White Sky Rock off the spur trail with great views of Caribou Lake. At main SHT, go left (east) 0.8 miles through maple forest and cross Caribou Trail once more.

1.6 (9.4) Caribou Trail

SHT crosses ditch, passes boardwalk and wet spots, and climbing wall of the Cathedral of the Pines camp. Trail crosses Co. Rd. 39. This land all belongs to camp, so please stay on trail. Steep climb through big cedar and maple to ridge with vista of Caribou Lake. Many trails that are part of camp cross SHT. SHT travels through maple forest, with maples turning to alder thicket as trail approaches Jonvick Creek and crosses small plank bridges.

3.0 (8.0) Jonvick Creek Campsite and beaver dam

▲ Jonvick Creek Campsite

Tent pads: 2
Water: From beaver pond
Setting: On beaver pond
Previous campsite: 2.4 miles
Next campsite: 2.2 miles

Cross boardwalk built on top of beaver dam. Immediately after dam, SHT crosses a wide, grassy snowmobile trail, then meanders through mixed forest. SHT crosses ski trail from Solbakken Resort, then ascends gentle slope through mature aspen to maple grove and views of Lake Superior on top of ridge. SHT goes through spruce plantation with wide views of Lake Superior, crosses two dirt roads (one called Hall Rd.), then reenters maples. SHT continues along ridgeline in cedar, birch, and pine, with views of inland ridges, then descends sharply to Spruce Creek. As with other ridges on SHT, hawks are visible from this ridge during fall migration.

5.2 (5.8) Spruce Creek Campsite

▲ Spruce Creek Campsite

Tent pads: 7
Water: From Spruce Creek
Setting: In large cedar grove
Previous campsite: 2.2 miles
Next campsite: 3.3 miles

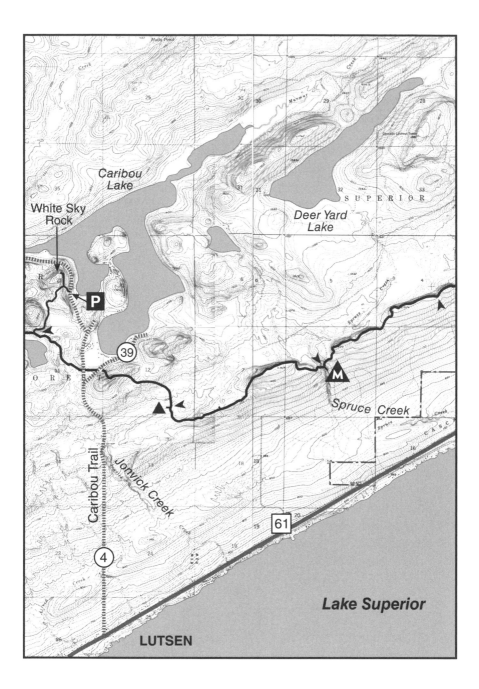

White Sky
Rock

Caribou
Lake

Deer Yard
Lake

S U P E R I O R

P

39

O R E

Spruce Creek

Caribou Trail

Jonvick Creek

4

61

Lake Superior

LUTSEN

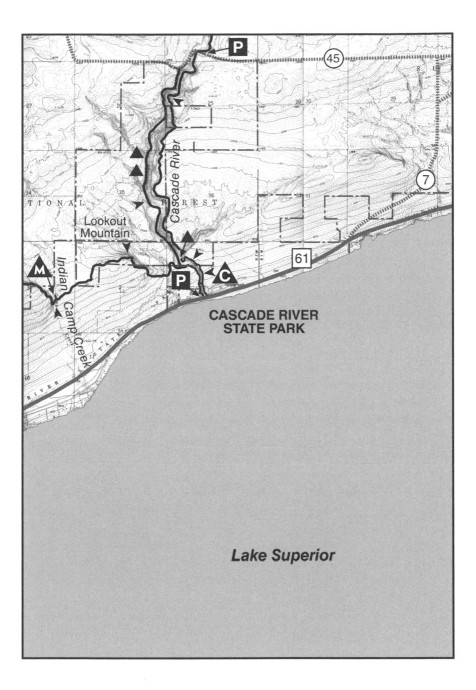

CASCADE RIVER
STATE PARK

Lake Superior

After campsite, SHT ascends to ridgeline of birch, spruce, fir, cedar, and pine. SHT crosses snowmobile trail to another ridgeline with views of Lake Superior and inland ridges, then slopes down to open, sometimes muddy area and back up to another ridgeline with almost pure maple. This area was hit by a huge windstorm in 2009.

6.8 (4.2) Junction with snowmobile trail
SHT uses wider snowmobile trail for 0.5 miles, continuing up and down along grassy, open ridge. Watch carefully as SHT leaves snowmobile trail sharply to left, then climbs ridge to view of inland ridges and the lakeshore toward Grand Marais, before steeply descending along curving ridgeline and cliff edge, past 10-yard spur to viewpoint.

8.5 (2.5) Indian Camp Creek

⚠ Indian Camp Creek Campsite

Tent pads: 6
Water: From Indian Camp Creek
Setting: In woods, surrounded by windblown trees
Previous campsite: 3.3 miles
Next campsite: 3.3 miles if following west side of Cascade River; 3.2 miles if following east side of Cascade River (or use Cascade River State Park campground)

After campsite, SHT crosses a snowmobile trail, meanders through woods of cedar, birch, and aspen, then down to wooden walkways across potentially muddy area. SHT then climbs through aspen woods, meets state park ski trail and follows this trail to junction with state park fee campsite. SHT continues up to Lookout Mountain overlook.

9.7 (1.3) Lookout Mountain
Benches and a trail register at overlook. SHT descends, crossing ski trail to Cascade Lodge. SHT passes large stumps left over from white pine logging, then crosses another ski trail. SHT crosses Cascade Creek, and then joins Cascade River State Park trail. SHT turns (left) soon after crossing creek. Watch for signed trail junction at top of the famous "96 Steps."

10.5 (0.5) Trail Junction at 96 Steps

Main SHT does not descend 96 Steps but takes slight left onto state park foot trail and continues downhill to footbridge over Cascade River. Main SHT crosses on bridge and ascends east of river. At footbridge, spur trail continues downhill to wayside parking lot.

At junction with 96 steps, to continue up west side of river either on Cascade River Loop or to go to Co. Rd. 45 by the shortest route, descend steps, turn left and follow river upstream (north).

10.8 (0.2) Cascade River bridge
Spur trails to the Hwy. 61 parking lot go down both sides of the river.

11.0 (0.0) Cascade River Wayside parking lot

Trail Maintenance Volunteers

Is the trail too muddy for your tastes? Are more boardwalks needed? Is there a newly fallen tree that needs to be cut? The Superior Hiking Trail is maintained by us, the trail users. If you or your group would like to lend a helping hand, let us know. Contact the SHTA to volunteer.

Cascade River State Park to Bally Creek Road
9.5 miles

Section description: Cascade River Wayside on Hwy. 61 to Forest Rd. 158 (Bally Creek Rd.)

Access and parking: *Directions to beginning trailhead:* At Hwy. 61 milepost 99.9 on left side of highway. Main SHT is on the east side of the river and remains closer to the river. Spur trail on west side of river starts near river and then travels away from river through mature maple forest. There is a bridge upstream 0.2 miles from the wayside parking lot to cross from one side of the river to the other. No overnight parking is allowed at the wayside. Overnight parking is available at Cascade River State Park. Continue on Hwy. 61 about a mile further to reach the state park main entrance. Check in at visitor center to be directed to parking area. A 0.25-mile spur trail goes from parking area to trail on east side of river. State park sticker required.

There are two additional parking options: 1) Co. Rd. 45 (Pike Lake Rd.) on north end of Cascade River loop. At Hwy. 61 milepost 101.5, turn left on Co. Rd. 7 and go 2.0 miles to junction with Cook Co. Rd. 44. Continue straight on Co. Rd. 44 for 0.5 miles. Turn left and go on Co. Rd. 45 for 2.6 miles to parking lot on right. Overnight parking okay.

2) Co. Rd. 158 (Bally Creek Rd.) at the Sundling Creek spur trail. At Hwy. 61 milepost 101.7, turn left (north) on Co. Rd. 7 and go 4.3 miles. Turn left on Co. Rd. 48 and go 0.3 miles to "T" intersection. Turn left on Forest Rd. 158 (Bally Creek Rd.) and go 1.1 miles (passing first SHT parking lot on Bally Creek Road) to large grassy parking lot on left. Overnight parking okay.

Facilities at starting trailhead: none

Designated campsites on this section: five

Synopsis: After ascending the scenic Cascade River valley, this section of the SHT travels through spruce-fir-aspen forests. The 7.8-mile Cascade River loop is a challenging but rewarding hike, up one side of the river and down the other side.

Mile-by-Mile Description

0.0 (9.5) Trailhead
Spur trail to main SHT is on east side of Hwy. 61 bridge over Cascade River, behind the guard rail. Spur trail climbs up steps. Look for Cascade Falls below.

0.2 (9.3) Junction at footbridge
At this junction SHT goes up either the west or east side of the Cascade River. This is a popular 7.8-mile loop hike up one side and down the other.

Following east side of Cascade River

From bridge above gorgeous waterfalls SHT passes spur from state park campground. Trail climbs steeply, then levels off. SHT follows state park hiking/ski trail and then descends steeply to Trout Creek, crosses long bridge and passes campsite.

1.3 (8.2) Trout Creek Campsite

▲ Trout Creek Campsite

Tent pads: 5
Water: From Cascade River
Setting: Near confluence of Trout Creek and Cascade River, on steep creek bank
Previous campsite (Indian Creek Campsite): 3.2 miles
Next campsite: 3.7 miles

After campsite, SHT follows bluff above river, with occasional views and sounds of river below. Note how tree mix along river differs from that along bluff.

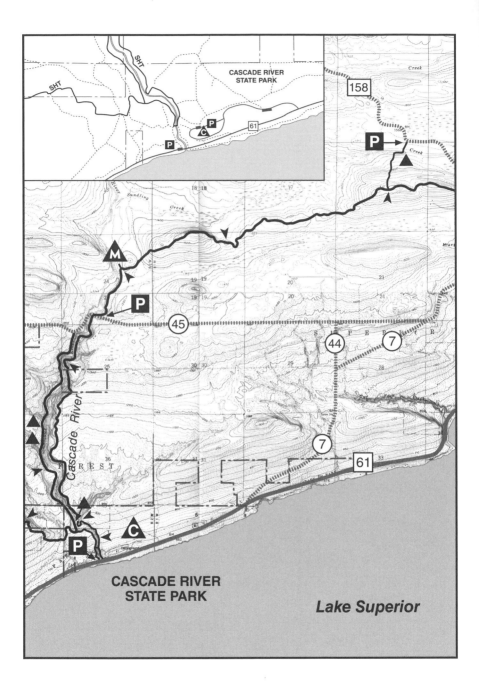

CASCADE RIVER STATE PARK

Lake Superior

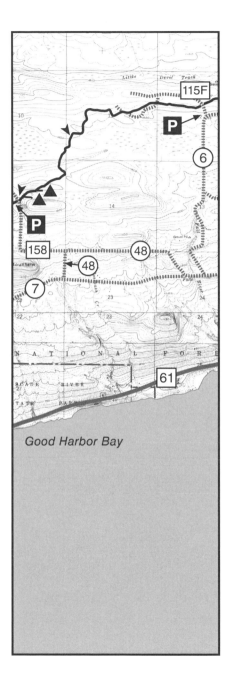

Good Harbor Bay

Cascade River State Park

Named for the series of stair-step-ping waterfalls on the Cascade River, Cascade River State Park offers numerous spectacular views along trails and bridges that follow and cross the river. Its 2,865 acres follow a half-mile-wide band along 1.5 miles of Lake Superior shoreline. Cascade served as an Emergency Conservation Work (ECW) camp during the 1930s. Their handi-work includes the trails that follow the river. Within the park are eighteen miles of hiking trails, many of which connect with the Superior Hiking Trail and other trails in the Superior National Forest. Located within the park is an enclosed picnic shelter, a mod-ern campground with 40 drive-in sites, two group camp sites, and five backpack sites, one located on the Lake Superior shore. A small picnic area is also located along Lake Superior.

3.2 (6.3) SHT returns to river

SHT makes steep descent to river's edge, climbs bluff, and makes another steep descent to river. The east side of the Cascade is very slippery when wet so use caution when hiking. Trail continues along river through cedar, pine, alder and birch.

3.9 (5.6) Co. Rd. 45 and parking lot

SHT passes under bridge, into parking lot, and continues upstream from parking lot. If hiking the Cascade River loop, walk 0.3 miles west (left, across the bridge) on Co. Rd. 45 to the next trailhead sign. This area had a CCC camp in the early 1930s. If continuing on, main SHT travels gradually along ridge, descends to cross Minnow Trap Creek and then climbs steps to follow top of bluff along Cascade River. Note views of river and ridges to northwest.

Following west side of Cascade River (SHT spur trail)

After footbridge over falls, SHT spur trail climbs gradually along river. At junction with 96 steps, spur trail does not climb steps but continues upstream along river and then gradually leaves river. Large cedars dominate on this stretch of trail and the treadway is rocky and full of roots.

▲ Big White Pine Campsite

Tent pads: 3
Water: From small tributary of Cascade River
Setting: In grove of white pine trees
Previous campsite: 3.3 miles (or use State Park)
Next campsite: 0.5 miles

2.3 (7.2) Cut Log Campsite

After SHT crosses 25-foot bridge, trail comes to Cut Log Campsite. Check out remains of two very large white pines cut by loggers many years ago and left behind. One of these logs, at the edge of campsite, is nearly four feet in diameter.

▲ Cut Log Campsite

Tent pads: 3
Water: From small creek below campsite
Setting: In woods, away from Cascade River
Previous campsite: 0.5 miles
Next campsite (on west side of river): 2.3 miles

SHT continues through old-growth maple forest. Catch some outstanding views of the Cascade River just before SHT reaches Co. Rd. 45.

3.6 (5.9) Junction with Co. Rd. 45

Turn right and follow Co. Rd. 45 0.3 miles to junction with east side trail at parking lot. This ends west side trail. Hikers can now either return to Hwy. 61 on the east side going downstream (right turn) or go on to Bally Creek going upstream.

4.6 (4.9) North Cascade River Campsite

▲ North Cascade River Campsite

Tent pads: 6
Water: From Cascade River
Setting: On hill above river
Previous campsite: 2.3 miles on west side of Cascade River or
   3.7 miles on east side of Cascade River
Next campsite: 4.3 miles

After campsite spur, SHT turns sharply northeast and moves away from river. Trail climbs gradually, passing through alder thickets and through stand of red pine whose needles carpet the ground to reach ridge overlooking Sundling Creek valley. Eagle Mountain, the highest point in Minnesota, is visible from here. Note views across valley to north. SHT descends past series of cross trails and steps to ski trail.

6.0 (3.5) Ski trail

After crossing ski trail, SHT climbs low ridge and then climbs another ridge with views back to Lake Superior. Trail continues along several ridges though mixed forest to high point on ridge.

Geology of North Shore Waterfalls

The North Shore is blessed by many beautiful waterfalls, including several that give the name to the Cascade River. The abundance of waterfalls is basically the result of two factors: 1) the profound erosion of the Lake Superior basin by the great Ice Age glaciers, which led to the steep slope of the North Shore; and 2) the occurrence of hard igneous rocks underlying the coastal zone. The fast-running rivers have eroded the softer bedrock to form the deeper parts of the gorges. However, the bedrock has some harder parts, such as dikes or the lower parts of lava flows, and these resist erosion, leading to falls and cascades. Many of the falls on the Cascade River represent individual basalt lava flows.

8.4 (1.1) Spur trail

Spur trail goes north 0.7 miles to additional parking lot on Forest Rd. 158 (Bally Creek Rd.) Spur trail goes through birch forest, crosses a low area, climbs a low ridge, passes campsite, and descends to Sundling Creek. Spur crosses creek, then follows a rise into parking lot.

▲ Sundling Creek Campsite

Tent pads: 4
Water: From Sundling Creek
Setting: Above Sundling Creek
Previous campsite: 4.3 miles
Next campsite: 1.7 miles

After spur trail, main SHT continues along ridgeline through hardwoods with many views to north. SHT begins gradual descent through stand of red pine, then continues descent to Forest Rd. 158 (Bally Creek Rd.) parking lot.

9.5 (0.0) Bally Creek Rd. trailhead parking lot

Bally Creek Road to Grand Marais
8.3 miles

Section description: Forest Rd. 158 (Bally Creek Rd.) to Pincushion Mountain trailhead on Cook Co. Rd. 53 (Pincushion Dr.)

Access and parking: *Directions to beginning trailhead:* At Hwy. 61 milepost 101.7, turn left (north) on Cook Co. Rd. 7 and go 4.3 miles. Turn left on Cook Co. Rd. 48 and go 0.3 miles to a "T" intersection. Turn left on Forest Rd. 158 (Bally Creek Rd.) and go 1.0 mile to trailhead parking lot on left. Overnight parking okay.

There is one other parking option: There is a parking lot on Forest Rd. 115F off Co. Rd. 6 3.1 miles from beginning of section. To get to parking lot, at Hwy. 61 milepost 101.7, turn left (north) on Cook Co. Rd. 7 and go 6.0 miles. Turn left on Cook Co. Rd. 6 and go 1.5 miles to pull-through parking lot at intersection with 115F. Watch carefully for sign. Overnight parking okay.

Facilities at starting trailhead: none

Designated campsites on this section: two

Synopsis: The western half of this section is marked by a large beaver pond and Sundling Creek. The SHT passes through a large red pine forest before it joins the North Shore State Trail for 2.5 miles. There is a steep descent from the ridgeline with lake views heading into the Pincushion Mtn. parking lot.

Mile-by-Mile Description

0.0 (8.3) Trailhead parking lot
The first campsite spur is only 0.2 miles into the hike.

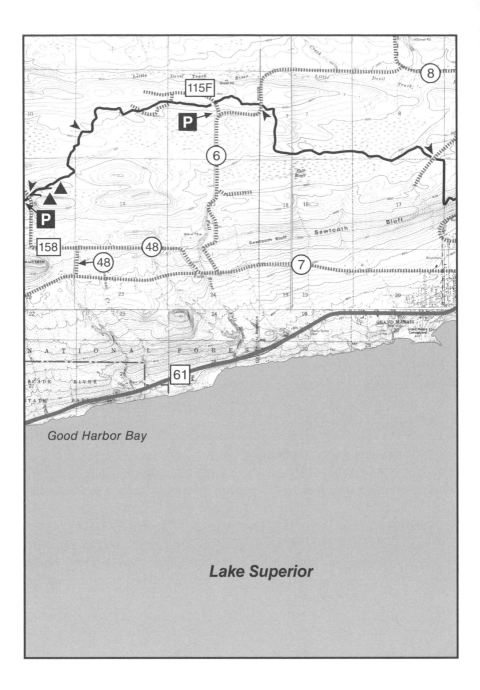

Good Harbor Bay

Lake Superior

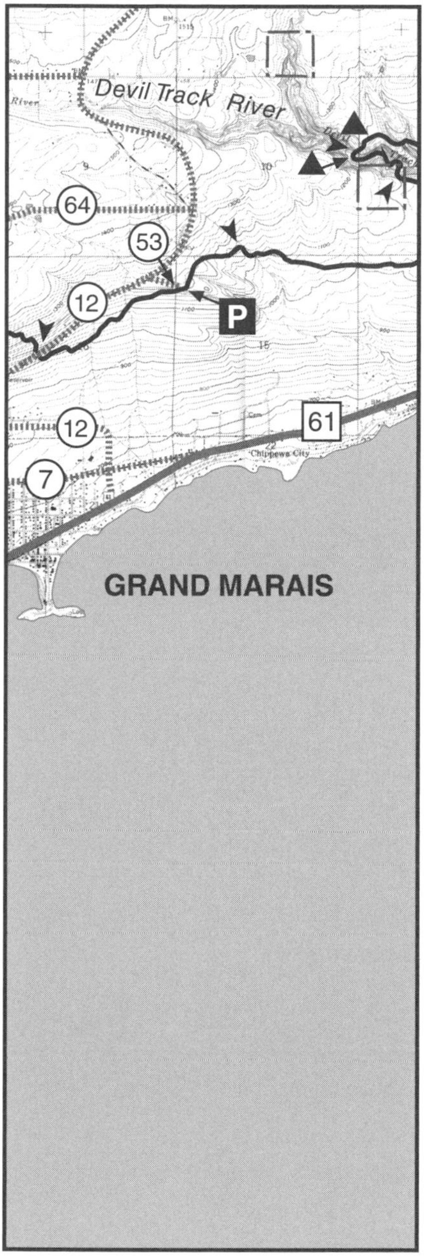

▲ South Bally Creek Pond Campsite

Tent pads: 4
Water: From beaver pond
Setting: On beaver pond
Previous campsite: 1.7 miles
Next campsite: 0.2 miles

SHT crosses a 13-foot bridge over small creek that drains beaver pond and travels along pond.

▲ North Bally Creek Pond Campsite

Tent pads: 3
Water: From beaver pond
Setting: On beaver pond
Previous campsite: 0.2 miles
Next campsite: 10.5 miles

SHT climbs away from pond into mixed deciduous forest, then gradually descends to Sundling Creek pond through pines. Find a rest bench to the right at the pond.

0.8 (7.5) Sundling Creek dam

SHT follows 193-foot boardwalk over beaver dam. Trail ascends back into mixed conifers and aspen. Trail comes to wet area with 15-foot bridge over small creek and then enters aspen forest.

2.1 (6.2) West crossing of Forest Rd. 115F

SHT crosses 115F three times within a mile. Trail soon enters one of largest red pine forests on entire length of trail, planted in 1937. At third of three crossings, at 3.1 (5.2), a spur trail heads 0.1 miles south to Cook Co. Rd. 6 and parking lot. Main SHT continues east.

3.7 (4.6) Cook Co. Rd. 6 crossing
SHT crosses road and continues 0.2 miles to North Shore State Trail. SHT follows North Shore State Trail for next 2.5 miles. The North Shore State Trail is a wider path used by snowmobiles and the John Beargrease Sled Dog Race in winter. Trail passes through very wet areas and gradually rises to drier area bordered by mixed forest.

6.3 (2.0) Cook Co. Rd. 64 (Tower Rd.)
Radio and television transmitters are visible to right. SHT crosses road and shortly leaves North Shore State Trail on right and heads toward Grand Marais with Lake Superior gradually becoming visible. SHT traverses long wet area on boardwalk. As SHT descends, the lake becomes more visible. Trail comes to views of Lake Superior and then descends steeply.

7.3 (1.0) Gunflint Trail (Co. Rd. 12) crossing
No parking here, but road edge is wide and safe. This is the closest access to Grand Marais for services. SHT crosses road and goes uphill, eventually joining a ski trail. SHT continues uphill, crosses the North Shore State Trail and comes to dramatic views at Pincushion Mountain trailhead.

8.3 (0.0) Pincushion Mountain trailhead parking lot

Grand Marais to Cook County Road 58
4.9 miles

Section description: Pincushion Mountain trailhead on Co. Rd. 53 (Pincushion Dr.) off Co. Rd. 12 (Gunflint Trail) to Cook Co. Rd. 58 (Lindskog Rd.)

Access and parking: *Directions to beginning trailhead:* At Hwy. 61 mile-post 110.0, turn left on Cook Co. Rd. 12 (Gunflint Trail) and go 2.0 miles. Turn right on Cook Co. Rd. 53 (Pincushion Drive) and go 0.25 miles to parking lot. Turn from Gunflint Trail has sign marked "Scenic Overlook." Overnight parking okay.

Facilities at starting trailhead: outhouse

Designated campsites on this section: two

Synopsis: This section offers a must-see spur to a panoramic vista at the summit of Pincushion Mountain. The trail then descends and climbs out of the Devil Track River gorge and follows the canyon edge to the end of the section.

Mile-by-Mile Description

0.0 (4.9) Pincushion Mountain trailhead
This is a popular trailhead for cross-country skiing, with 25 kilometers of groomed trails. The SHT follows ski trails for 2.2 miles. You must stay off groomed trails in winter.

0.4 (4.5) Junction #4
SHT turns right here and travels along ski trail through mixed forest and several small creeks.

Cross Country Skiing and the North Shore Snowbelt

At numerous places, the Superior Hiking Trail intersects or shares its route with a cross-country ski trail. Ski trails are wider than the hiking trail, tend to be grassy, and often have blue diamonds marking their course. The winter skier can have an experience similar to that of the summer hiker, with the same beautiful forests, dramatic overlooks and ease of access. There is an extensive network of trails that link all parts of the North Shore. The winter experience is made all the more enjoyable by the generally ample snow, created by the lake-effect snowfall along the North Shore ridgeline. It's not unusual to have two feet of snow inland and none along the highway. Note: if snowshoeing the SHT in winter, please stay off of any groomed ski track.

1.7 (3.2) Spur trail to Pincushion Mountain summit

0.25-mile spur trail to summit with sweeping vistas of Grand Marais, Sawtooth Mountains, Lake Superior, and Devil Track River valley.

2.2 (2.7) Junction of ski trail and SHT

SHT departs ski trail and descends over 200 feet down to Devil Track River along 150 steps.

2.5 (2.4) Devil Track River Bridge

This 50-foot "A"-shape bridge was built in summer of 1992. The canyon is deep and remote. Campsites on both west and east side of river.

▲ West Devil Track Campsite

Tent pads: 6
Water: From Devil Track River
Setting: On west bank of river
Previous campsite: 10.5 miles
Next campsite: 0.1 miles

▲ East Devil Track Campsite

Tent pads: 2
Water: From Devil Track River
Setting: On east bank of river
Previous campsite: 0.1 miles
Next campsite: 2.9 miles

SHT climbs steeply uphill from campsite, about 0.2 miles to

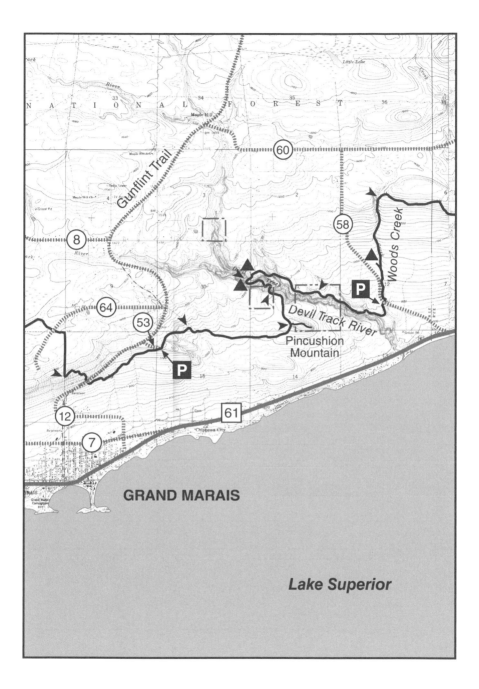

GRAND MARAIS

Lake Superior

Spruce Knob, then continues along canyon's edge, crossing bridges at 2.9 and 3.5 miles. Watch for scenic waterfalls and gorgeous red cliffs below.

3.9 (1.0) Barrier Falls overlook

After the overlook, SHT passes 1937 tree plantation marker and eventually descends steps to cross stream on bridge. Trail continues through aspen, birch, and pine. A fisherman's trail crosses the SHT and heads straight down to river. About 0.2 miles from parking lot is the last (or first) good overlook on canyon.

4.9 (0.0) Cook Co. Rd. 58 (Lindskog Rd.) trailhead parking lot

Cook County Road 58
to Kadunce River Wayside
9.2 miles

Section description: Cook Co. Rd. 58 (Lindskog Rd.) to Kadunce River Wayside on Hwy. 61

Access and parking: *Directions to beginning trailhead:* At Hwy. 61 milepost 113.8, turn left and go 0.8 miles to trailhead parking lot on left. Overnight parking okay.

There is another parking option: There is another parking option at Cook Co. Rd. 14, 6.8 miles from the start of the section. At Hwy. 61 milepost 117.6, turn left and go 0.7 miles to parking lot. Overnight parking okay.

Facilities at starting trailhead: none

Designated campsites on this section: six

Synopsis: There are a number of unusual features to this section of the SHT. The section begins and ends with intimate streams, from the gentle gurgle of Woods Creek to the deep gorges of the Kadunce River, which offer a fascinating glimpse into the region's geology. The middle part of the section takes you across a unique high, wet area with many footbridges. Trees on this section include oak and black spruce.

Mile-by-Mile Description

0.0 (9.2) Parking lot on Co. Rd. 58
SHT crosses Co. Rd. 58 and then follows Woods Creek through birch, aspen and ash. Sharp-edged red rock is rhyolite. Trail then goes through dark spruces with old man's beard (a lichen) drooping from branches.

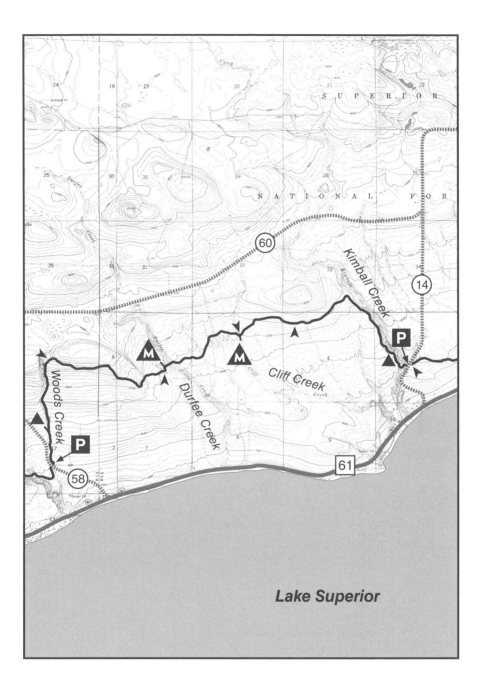

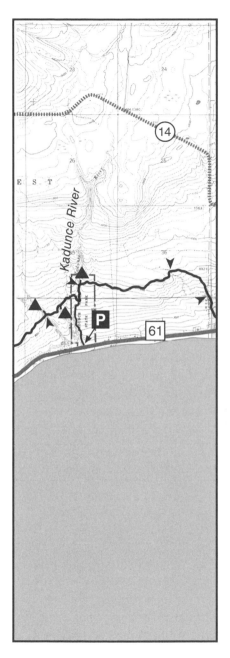

▲ Wood's Creek Campsite

Tent pads: 4
Water: From Woods Creek
Setting: On creek
Previous campsite: 2.9 miles
Next campsite: 2.4 miles

1.2 (8.0) SHT leaves creek

SHT turns east and climbs into parklike aspen and birch forest, then a series of previously logged areas and nice open field (SHT marked by rock cairns). Views of Lake Superior, Pincushion Mountain at first, then wide view southwest of Pincushion, Maple Hill radio tower, and Sawtooth range. Birches gradually give way to aspens. In open area, watch for bluebirds in field and Five-Mile Rock in Lake Superior. At far side of field, SHT enters a mixed woods, crosses ATV trail, passes through a wildlife opening, and then goes through spruce plantation.

3.0 (6.2) Durfee Creek Campsite

▲ Durfee Creek Campsite

Tent pads: 6
Water: From Durfee Creek
Setting: In woods
Previous campsite: 2.4 miles
Next campsite: 1.1 miles

After campsite, SHT crosses a series of plank bridges in this up-and-down section, with lots of white spruce and old burned stumps.

4.1 (5.1) Cliff Creek Campsite
Woods become more mixed, with birch, aspen and fir. Lake Superior comes into view, the sharp, red rhyolite returns underfoot, and there are occasional vistas.

⚠ Cliff Creek Campsite

Tent pads: 8
Water: From Cliff Creek
Setting: In woods
Previous campsite: 1.1 miles
Next campsite: 2.6 miles

5.1 (4.1) Scrub oak overlook
Expansive view of Lake Superior. On SHT look for unusual small oak trees in field and large (30-inch diameter) aspens. SHT begins to follow Kimball Creek in towering cedar forest, crosses creek, and crosses Kimball Creek Trail (an unmaintained fishing trail along the river). SHT then crosses small tributary and climbs steep steps. The bridge on Kimball Creek is one of the most picturesque settings on trail.

▲ Kimball Creek Campsite

Tent pads: 3
Water: From Kimball Creek
Setting: At base of hill past creek
Previous campsite: 2.6 miles
Next campsite: 1.2 miles

6.8 (2.4) Cook Co. Rd. 14
SHT crosses road at parking lot and climbs through cutover area, then passes under powerline before entering woods. After view of Lake Superior, SHT descends. Look for bunchberry and thimbleberry. SHT crosses couple of footpaths and small opening. Trail is mostly rock here. SHT descends steps to Crow Creek.

▲ Crow Creek Campsite

Tent pads: 4
Water: From Crow Creek, un reliable in dry conditions
Setting: In wooded area above canyon on Crow Creek
Previous campsite: 1.2 miles
Next campsite: 0.4 miles

7.9 (1.3) Crow Creek

This stream has steep rock walls upstream from the bridge. SHT climbs out of creek drainage, crosses a footpath, then comes to another narrow steep canyon, the west branch of Kadunce River. Watch for bearing tree right before crossing.

▲ West Fork of the Kadunce Campsite

Tent pads: 4
Water: Stream is mostly dry and hard to get to;
   use Kadunce River (0.5 miles)
Setting: In wooded area above canyon on west branch of
   Kadunce River
Previous campsite: 0.4 miles
Next campsite: 0.5 miles

8.5 (0.7) Kadunce River

After crossing bridge, spur trail goes downstream 0.7 miles to Hwy. 61. Spur follows river until river drops into gorge, then rejoins river after gorge. The canyon is very deep yet only about eight feet wide in places.

9.2 (0.0) Kadunce River Wayside on Hwy. 61

Kadunce River Wayside to Judge Magney State Park

10.0 miles

Section description: Kadunce River Wayside on Hwy. 61 to Judge C.R. Magney State Park

Access and parking: *Directions to beginning trailhead:* At Hwy. 61 milepost 119 on right side of highway. Overnight parking is not allowed.

Facilities at starting trailhead: none

Designated campsites on this section of trail: four

Synopsis: This is an exciting section of the SHT, since it is the only part that is directly on the Lake Superior shoreline. It also passes through many different stages of tree succession following logging in the area, and some classic North Shore river gorges, including the Kadunce River.

Mile-by-Mile Description

0.0 (10.0) Kadunce River Wayside
SHT crosses Hwy. 61 and goes past trailhead sign. The spectacular 0.7-mile spur trail begins climbing almost immediately along the edge of the Kadunce River gorge, which is pocked by occasional "swirl caves" created at various stages of the gorge's creation. Spur trail meets the main SHT at bridge crossing the Kadunce River.

0.7 (9.3) Bridge over Kadunce River
Spur trail joins main SHT here. Main SHT veers right and continues upstream on same side of river, climbs hill and passes campsite, climbs again and then leaves river. Forest changes from birch and fir to dense, relatively younger aspen. SHT crosses old grassy logging roadbed and then two footpaths.

▲ Kadunce River Campsite

Tent pads: 3
Water: From Kadunce River
Setting: In woods, close to Kadunce River
Previous campsite: 0.5 miles
Next campsite: 5.3 miles

2.0 (8.0) Blueberry Overlook
SHT follows rock cairns through open area that leads to overlook with expansive view of Lake Superior. SHT crosses stream and enters mixed woods. Trail then enters another logged area replanted with spruce, with large white pines left standing. Trail descends and passes many raspberry patches in a young aspen forest.

2.7 (7.3) Kelly's Hill Rd.
SHT crosses road (note SHT sign), then descends through scrubby woods, dense young aspen stand and mixed woods.

3.2 (6.8) Hwy. 61, west end of Lakewalk
SHT crosses Hwy. 61 to follow shore of Lake Superior on soft pebble beach. This is the only part of the SHT on Lake Superior. Here one can literally touch the many moods of this great lake. Notice the different surge levels up the beach from storms and wind, especially the unimpeded northeast winds. Look for bog areas between beach and Hwy. 61—good spring birding, as birds use shoreline for navigation. SHT turns inland just past a very small rock island barely off shore.

4.8 (5.2) Hwy. 61, east end of Lakewalk
After crossing Hwy. 61, SHT passes large birches and passes under powerline and through mixed woods along Hane Creek, crossing stream on small wood bridge after passing through low areas. SHT eventually climbs and passes large cedar and white pine and overlooks of waterfalls and pools on Little Brule River. SHT crosses river on bridge, ascends through mature aspen, then levels out.

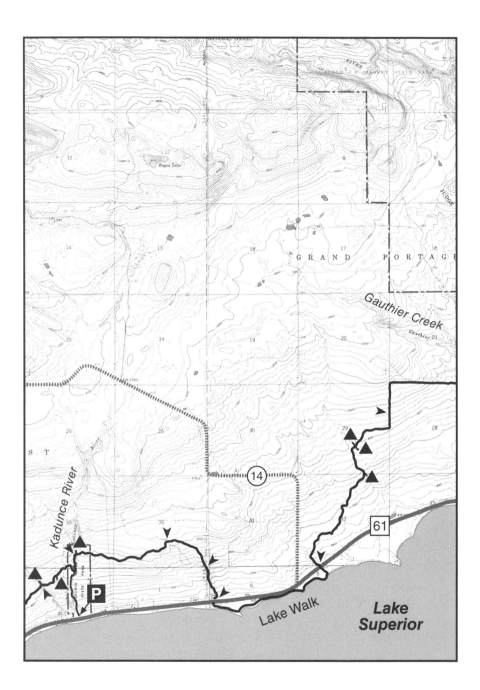

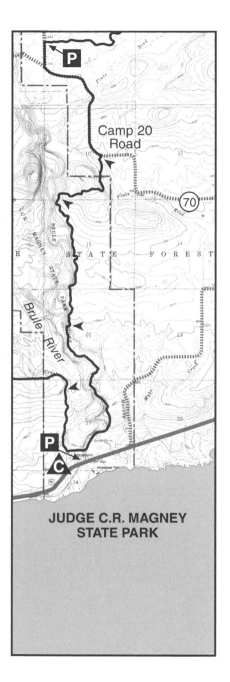

JUDGE C.R. MAGNEY
STATE PARK

▲ South Little Brule River Campsite

Tent pads: 2
Water: From river, unreliable in dry conditions
Setting: In woods
Previous campsite: 5.3 miles
Next campsite: 0.4 miles

▲ North Little Brule River Campsite

Tent pads: 4
Water: From river, unreliable in dry conditions
Setting: In woods
Previous campsite: 0.4 miles
Next campsite: 0.0 miles

▲ Northwest Little Brule River Campsite

Tent pads: 3
Water: From river, unreliable in dry conditions
Setting: In woods
Previous campsite: 0.0 miles
Next campsite: 11.9 miles (or use Judge C.R. Magney State Park)

7.1 (2.9) Gravel pit road
SHT winds through young aspen forest. Look for blueberries in open sections. For approximately 1.5 miles the SHT follows straight borderline of private property, past Lake Superior views and mature

Pebble Beaches

A beach must have both a source of rock particles and wave action to deposit and move the particles. Beaches continually change in reaction to changes in the waves from storm to calm to storm. Some of the smaller beaches on the North Shore are made of rocks ripped from the nearby bedrock ledges; larger beaches are made possible where the waves have access to more easily-eroded glacial deposits. The long, low beaches between Grand Marais and Hovland are made both from local volcanic rhyolite, which breaks up into easily erodible chips or shingles, and reworked older beach deposits from the Nipissing stage of Lake Superior, about 5000 years ago, when the lake was slightly higher and the beaches were on the other side of what is now the highway. Can you find any agates? They might have been brought by the ice sheet from Isle Royale or Canada.

pines. SHT crosses old road bed after a survey line, then follows Gauthier Creek.

9.1 (0.9) Junction with state park trail
As the trail begins to leave from Gauthier Creek, SHT joins state park ski trail and continues to parking lot.

10.0 (0.0) Judge C.R. Magney State Park trailhead parking lot
SHT enters parking lot located next to state park campground.

Judge Magney State Park to County Road 70

6.6 miles

Section description: Judge Magney State Park to Cook Co. Rd. 70 (Camp 20 Road)

Access and parking: *Directions to beginning trailhead:* At Hwy. 61 milepost 123.8, turn left into entrance for state park. Continue straight on service road to large parking lot. State park sticker required for entry to state park. Overnight parking okay.

There is an alternate parking option to avoid the 1.7 mile road walk at the end of this section: There is a large pull-off on the side of Co. Rd. 70 (Camp 20 Rd) where the trail comes to the road 4.9 miles from the start of the section. Parking is for day use only.

Facilities at starting trailhead: Outhouse, drinking water, picnic tables, campground

Designated campsites on this section: none; Judge Magney State Park has 36 fee campsites

Synopsis: In this section, the trail follows the Brule River for over two miles and features the dramatic Devil's Kettle Falls. The trail continues through mixed forest with occasional large cedars and white pine on the high bluff above the Brule River. The trail climbs to a rocky knob with a view of Lake Superior then descends into the picturesque Flute Reed River valley.

Mile-by-Mile Description

0.0 (6.6) Judge Magney State Park parking lot

SHT goes east (to the right) out of parking lot and crosses Brule River on 76-foot bridge by picnic tables and pit toilet. Trail continues

Judge C.R. Magney State Park

Judge C.R. Magney State Park is named after the former Minnesota Supreme Court Justice Clarence R. Magney. A strong advocate of Minnesota state parks, he was instrumental in establishing eleven parks and waysides along the North Shore. This park was established in 1957 to preserve three waterfalls on the Brule River: the Lower Falls, the Upper Falls, and the Devil's Kettle. The Devil's Kettle was named appropriately. A large rock juts out and splits the river in two. The east branch drops 50 feet to a deep gorge and pool. The west branch plunges into a huge pothole and, according to legend, disappears forever. 4,674 acres in size, today the park has nine miles of trail and 36 campsites.

on bluff along Brule River with occasional dramatic overlooks and views of Lower and Upper Falls.

1.0 (5.6) Devil's Kettle Falls
SHT goes to overlook of Devil's Kettle Falls, one of the most dramatic falls on trail. Trail continues upstream along the river through beautiful forest of white pine, cedar, balsam fir, birch, spruce and aspen. Watch for occasional blackened tree stumps and cut stumps showing past history of forest.

2.0 (4.6) SHT leaves Brule River
SHT leaves Brule River at bottom of a hill with two benches and continues through forest on high bluff parallel to river.

2.8 (3.8) Large white pine
SHT passes large white pine on right with occasional large white pine scattered throughout forest.

3.9 (2.7) Rocky knob
SHT climbs to rocky knob covered with reindeer lichen. Look for views of Lake Superior. Trail continues along rocky outcrops; watch for cairns marking trail. Trail crosses private road—please stay on trail. Trail descends steeply and travels on private land through alder, ash, aspen and balsam forest.

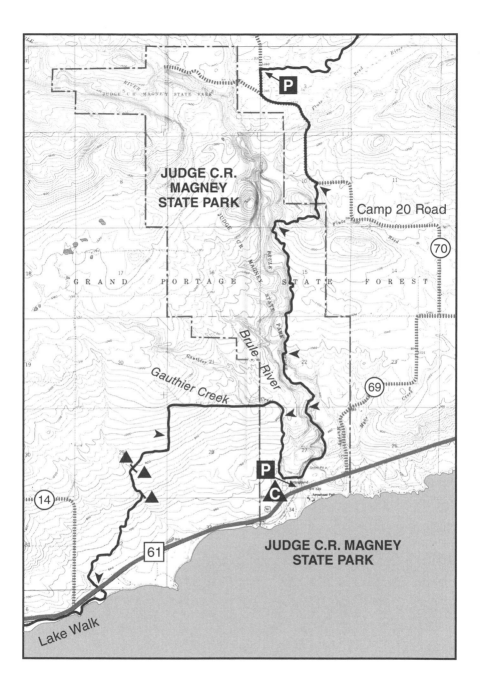

4.8 (1.8) Flute Reed River Bridge and beginning of road walk on Camp 20 Rd.

SHT crosses Flute Reed River, still on private land, and continues 300 feet to Co. Rd. 70 (Camp 20 Rd.). Trail continues on Co. Rd. 70 (Camp 20 Rd.) 1.7 miles north to parking lot. Note: Okay to park on the south side of Co. Rd. 70 (Camp 20 Rd.) by the Flute Reed River bridge for day hikes only. No overnight parking here.

6.6 (0.0) Trailhead parking lot on Camp 20 Rd. (Co. Rd. 70)

Absolutely no parking on road if parking lot is full. There is heavy truck traffic on this road.

County Road 70 to Arrowhead Trail
8.5 miles

SUPERIOR HIKING TRAIL

Section description: Co. Rd. 70 (Camp 20 Rd.) to Co. Rd. 16 (Arrowhead Trail)

Access and parking: *Directions to beginning trailhead:* At Hwy. 61 milepost 124.4, turn left (north) on Cook Co. Rd. 69 (North Rd.) and go 2.75 miles. Turn left (north) on Cook Co. Rd. 70 (Camp 20 Rd.) and go 4.75 miles to trailhead parking lot on right (about 0.25 miles past Hong Hill Rd.). Room for six cars only—absolutely no parking on road outside of parking lot since big logging trucks frequently use this narrow road. Overnight parking okay.

Facilities at starting trailhead: none

Designated campsites on this section: three

Synopsis: This section is in the Flute Reed and Carlson Creek watersheds. The large number of ponds in this section make it ideal for wildlife viewing, including waterfowl, beaver, and moose. There is a good deal of past and current beaver activity. This is an easier section of the trail.

Mile-by-Mile Description

0.0 (8.5) Co. Rd. 70 (Camp 20 Rd.) trailhead parking lot

Absolutely no parking on Camp 20 Rd. due to heavy equipment use of narrow road. SHT leaves parking lot and continues for 1.3 miles on private land. The first 0.25 miles is a mix of balsam poplar (also called Balm-of-Gilead), black ash, and tag alder. Trail comes into clearing where forest has been clearcut and replanted with spruce, white pine, and cedar so please stay on trail at all times. SHT passes islands

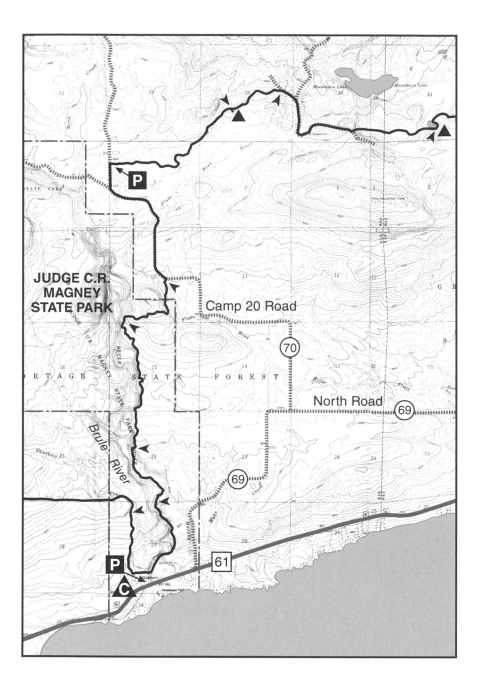

JUDGE C.R. MAGNEY STATE PARK

Camp 20 Road

70

North Road

69

Brule River

69

61

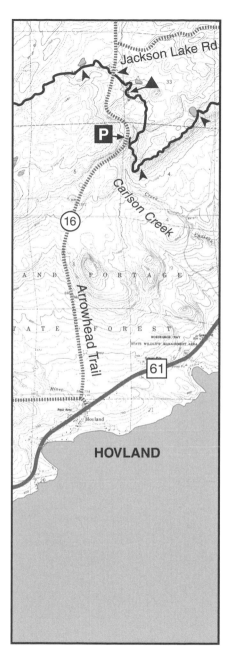

of mature spruce among planted trees. Watch for moose sign. Trail crosses two branches of Flute Reed River and also has nice view of pond where moose may occasionally be seen.

Note: If staying at the Hazel Campsite, second Flute Reed tributary crossing is water source for the campsite that is 1.8 miles farther on.

1.3 (7.2) Hazel corridor
SHT leaves private land and travels through a corridor of mixed forest with hazel predominating.

2.2 (6.3) Hazel Campsite

▲ Hazel Campsite

Tent pads: 3
Water: none (there may be a potential water source at tiny creek by curved ash tree 0.25 miles before campsite but don't rely on it). Get water from Flute Reed River branch, 1.8 miles before campsite
Setting: In brushy woods
Previous campsite: 11.9 miles; or 8.8 miles from Judge Magney State Park Campground
Next campsite: 3.0 miles

SHT continues through mixed forest of spruce, birch, balsam, aspen, alder, and ash. Trail rises steeply on old roadbed just before Tom Lake Rd. and SHT sign.

2.6 (5.9) Tom Lake Rd.
SHT turns right (east) and continues on Tom Lake Rd. for 1.3 miles. Numerous big white pine along road. Dogsledders also train along this road. Boyd Rd. is on left about 0.25 miles past trailhead sign. Moosehorn Lake Rd. is on the left 0.8 miles further on. Trail/road continues for another 0.25 miles then turns sharply uphill (left) at white pine ridge. Watch for SHT sign. SHT ascends hill on steep steps. Trail continues on hilltop through moss-covered blown-down trees. Note evidence of past fire in area. Trail continues through young sugar maple forest and then descends into birch, balsam, spruce, and aspen forest.

5.1 (3.4) Carlson Pond
SHT comes to Carlson Pond, a 200-300 acre beaver pond with two lobes. Balsam and spruce-covered islands dot pond. Watch for moose feeding in the pond. SHT continues along first lobe of pond, crosses Carlson Creek below pond on split log bridge and reaches second lobe.

▲ South Carlson Pond Campsite

Tent pads: 6
Water: From Carlson Pond
Setting: On pond
Previous campsite: 3.0 miles
Next campsite: 2.3 miles

SHT leaves pond and goes through mixed spruce, balsam, aspen, birch forest with occasional glimpses of ponds spread out along Carlson Creek. Trail comes to large pond by large spruce tree, a nice rest stop. Look for moose sign. Trail continues through mixed forest with board-walk in some areas.

6.5 (2.0) Old beaver pond
SHT crosses by old beaver pond and continues through mixed forest. Trail goes through red pine plantation and then along Carlson Creek until it reaches Co. Rd. 16 (Arrowhead Trail).

6.9 (1.6) Co. Rd. 16 (Arrowhead Trail) crossing

SHT continues on other side of road. No parking facilities here. SHT continues along Carlson Creek and comes to old beaver pond. Note huge 24-inch diameter aspen cut by beaver at campsite entrance.

7.4 (1.1) North Carlson Pond Campsite

▲ North Carlson Pond Campsite

Tent pads: 6
Water: From Carlson Creek/ Pond
Setting: On pond
Previous campsite: 2.3 miles
Next campsite: 4.1 miles

SHT continues by Carlson Creek through ash, aspen and alder forest and comes to huge spruce tree. After spruce tree, SHT ascends hill and continues through mixed forest. Trail crosses drainage and travels along ridge through balsam fir blowdown area, then descends steeply and goes along creek again to Carlson Creek bridge. Spur trail on other side of bridge goes steeply uphill to trailhead parking lot on Co. Rd. 16 (Arrowhead Trail). Main trail does not cross bridge but continues along creek.

8.5 (0.0) Co. Rd. 16 (Arrowhead Trail) parking lot

Fire Ecology

Forest fires, either by their absence or raging presence, have had significant impact on the forests of the North Shore. Fire is a natural part of many ecosystems, providing a periodic cleansing and an easy way to return nutrients to the soil. Many of the birch forests along the SHT grew up following large-scale forest fires that followed logging in the area—as evidence, look in the even-aged birch forests for the numerous large firecharred stumps of white pines. The few remaining patches of old-growth pines have likely survived a number of fires with their thick, corky bark and out-of-reach branches.

Arrowhead Trail to Jackson Lake Road
5.1 miles

Section description: Cook Co. Rd. 16 (Arrowhead Trail) to Jackson Lake Rd.

Access and parking: *Directions to beginning trailhead:* At Hwy. 61 milepost 128.9, turn left on Cook Co. Rd. 16 (Arrowhead Trail) and go 3.3 miles to trailhead parking lot on right. Overnight parking okay.

Facilities: at starting trailhead: none

Designated campsites on this section: one

Synopsis: This section is home to the ghost of the woodland caribou, which once roamed this part of Minnesota. Moss-covered rocks and lichen-draped trees give this land a true boreal feel. Experience the variety as the SHT winds from open rocky ridges with wide views of Lake Superior and Isle Royale into dark forests and quiet backwaters. One-half of this section follows an open rocky ridge with nearly continuous views.

Mile-by-Mile Description

0.0 (5.1) Parking lot on Arrowhead Trail
SHT spur trail departs from lot, descends steeply on steps to Carlson Creek, and crosses creek on 23-foot bridge. Main SHT continues along creek through alder before climbing steeply and continuing through large lichen-draped spruce.

0.6 (4.5) Southwest end of ridgetop
From first view through some young aspens, SHT meanders along this ridgeline for 1.5 miles. Cairns lead the way through mixed spruce, fir, and aspen forest as the views keep getting better. Look for Isle Royale over 20 miles away. Watch for beaver meadow as SHT nears a creek.

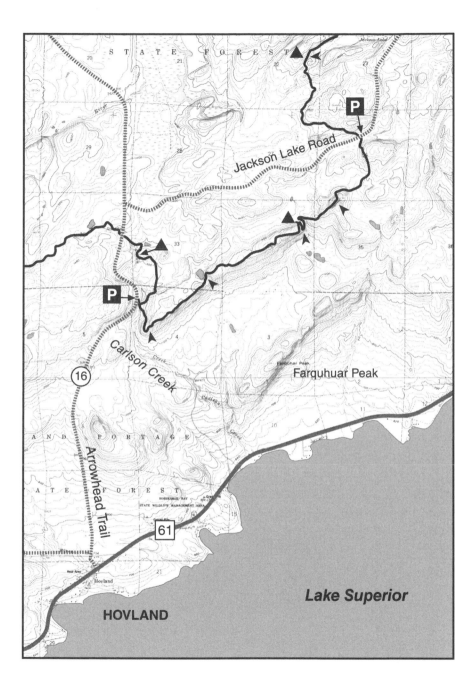

Lake Superior

HOVLAND

1.6 (3.5) Creek crossing

SHT crosses 24-foot bridge, skirts east edge of beaver meadow, and then climbs back to ridgetop through dead and dying fir. SHT descends steeply from ridge into valley, with nice views of beaver pond and Lake Superior below. SHT enters a dark forest, once the habitat of the woodland caribou, before meeting unnamed creek where the water appears to caress moss-covered boulders.

▲ Woodland Caribou Pond Campsite

Tent pads: 4
Water: From beaver pond
Setting: In woods overlooking old pond
Previous campsite: 4.0 miles
Next campsite: 3.8 miles

3.2 (1.9) Creek crossing

SHT crosses creek on bridge, near a couple of black ash, then climbs east side of creek and follows edge of beaver meadow. SHT climbs through a relatively mature mixed birch forest.

3.9 (1.2) Hellacious Overlook

Steep climb rewards hikers with a wide view of Lake Superior, Isle Royale, and beaver meadows below. SHT continues along ridgetop, with more views to the northeast, then descends steeply past dead and dying fir, into a wet area with alder and ash. SHT gradually climbs through aspen, birch and diseased fir, then descends steeply into a cedar swamp and across corduroy walkway to road. At Jackson Lake Rd., SHT turns right and follows road 350 feet to trailhead parking lot.

5.1 (0.0) Jackson Lake Rd. parking lot

Jackson Lake Road to Otter Lake Road

8.7 miles

Section description: Jackson Lake Rd. to Otter Lake Rd.

Access and parking: *Directions to beginning trailhead:* At Hwy. 61 milepost 128.9 turn left and go 4.5 miles on Co. Rd. 16 (Arrowhead Trail). Turn right on Jackson Lake Rd. and go 3.1 miles to trailhead parking lot on right. Overnight parking okay.

Directions to ending trailhead on Otter Lake Rd.: At Hwy. 61 milepost 128.9 turn left and go 4.5 miles on Co. Rd. 16 (Arrowhead Trail). Turn right on Jackson Lake Rd. and go 8.4 miles. Turn left on Otter Lake Rd. at Otter Lake Rd./Rengo Rd. "T" intersection and go 2.0 miles to trailhead parking lot on left.

Facilities at starting trailhead: none.

Facilities at ending trailhead: outhouse at Swamp River Public Access site and campsite (just past SHT parking lot)

Designated campsites on this section: two

Synopsis: This is the northernmost section of the trail. The trail reaches its highest elevation, 1,829 feet, on this section. Overlooks of Jackson Lake and the Swamp River drainage, and a spectacular maple forest on Sugarbush Ridge, are highlights. This is remote country, but with significant logging influence in the northern half.

Mile-by-Mile Description

0.0 (8.7) Jackson Lake Road

SHT follows Jackson Lake Rd. southwest for 350 feet and then turns right (northwest) into woods. Trail heads past 1997 logging area to first of several overlooks. Trail goes through mixed aspen, birch, spruce, and sugar maple with large cedar pockets.

1.0 (7.7) Descent to cedar swamp

SHT descends 600 feet down a steep side hill to reach Swamp River Pond and boardwalk through cedar swamp. Trail rises from swamp and comes to Jeremy's Rock, a large glacial erratic, and the Jackson Creek Pond campsite.

1.7 (7.0) Jackson Creek Pond Campsite

▲ Jackson Creek Pond Campsite

Tent pads: 3
Water: From Jackson Creek Pond; may be unreliable. Go upstream 100 yards on creek to deep pool on Jackson Creek.
Setting: On small beaver pond
Previous campsite: 3.8 miles
Next campsite: 5.3 miles

From Jackson Creek Pond SHT heads uphill and eastward to several partial overlooks above Jackson Lake. SHT drops off from Jackson Lake ridge into cedar forest on valley floor. It then climbs upward through beautiful old growth maple forest to several bedrock outcroppings on eastern face of SHT's highest hill. Before reaching high point, SHT turns onto north slope of hill, then climbs steeply to summit plateau.

3.8 (4.9) Highest point of trail, Rosebush Ridge

SHT reaches its highest point, 1,829 feet, in the midst of balsam forest. Watch for sign on tree. There is no view. Continuing west along summit plateau, views northward can be glimpsed through the trees. Raspberries grow profusely in this area. (The name Rosebush Ridge

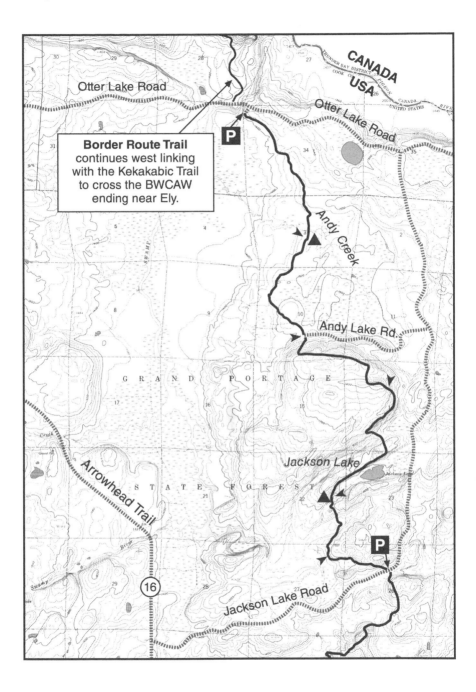

Otter Lake Road

Border Route Trail continues west linking with the Kekakabic Trail to cross the BWCAW ending near Ely.

CANADA
USA

THUNDER BAY DISTRICT
COOK CO.
CANADA
UNITED STATES

Otter Lake Road

Andy Creek

Andy Lake Rd.

GRAND PORTAGE

Arrowhead Trail

Jackson Lake

STATE FOREST

(16)

Jackson Lake Road

appears on some maps—apparently because an explorer was torn by thorns and did not properly identify the culprit species.) SHT descends steeply down to Andy Lake Rd.

5.3 (3.4) Andy Lake Road
The final section of trail from Andy Lake Rd. to Otter Lake Rd. is predominantly flat. Andy Lake Rd. is gated so there is no vehicle access. SHT passes through logged-over areas as well as open meadows of older logged areas. There are also pockets of large cedar throughout.

7.0 (1.7) Andy Creek Campsite and bridge

▲ Andy Creek Campsite

Tent pads: 4
Water: From Andy Creek
Setting: In woods close to Andy Creek
Previous campsite: 5.3 miles

SHT may be hard to follow if not recently weed-whipped in the meadow areas. Watch for blazes. SHT mostly follows old logging roads to the Otter Lake Rd.

8.7 (0.0) Otter Lake Rd. trailhead parking lot
This is the northern terminus of the Superior Hiking Trail. There is a public access site and campsite on the Swamp River about 300 feet west along the road. To continue to the Border Route Trail, go 0.2 miles west on the Otter Lake Rd. to the trailhead for the Border Route Trail.

A Final Note

The trouble is, we're tempted to think that a guided description can really describe and guide. Of course, no matter how well done, it cannot. It depends on what we're looking for.

The Superior Hiking Trail leads us from the mountain tops to the valley floors, to the deep woods and the cascading rivers. A guide can describe a rocky overlook at such and so, but it cannot tell whether it's fogged in or not.

And who's to say whether we find in the fog the mystery of the north woods, or whether we find disappointment in not seeing farther?

I'd like to pick a defining experience, a place and time on the trail where it all came together for me in some kind of mystical peak experience. The retelling of this, I believe, could show the true value of the trail. But would it really? We can wax poetically all we want about the North Shore and the ridgeline, and it will all be true. The truth is, the value we experience depends on what we're seeking.

Instead, for me, faces come to mind. It is the faces and personalities of all those who brought the trail to life with sweat and good humor. It is Mark, Duane, Bob, Cory, Toivo, Neil, Harry, Stormy, and forty others who did the actual work of trail building. It is John, Tom, Bill, and Anne who, by the force of their character, willed the trail into existence.

For this trail to be really worthwhile, it should be more than just fun. It should heighten our awareness and appreciation of all that is natural. It should make us realize our place in the diverse complex web that is the land. With a little luck and a little help it might, for a few of us. And that would be worthwhile.

— *Tom Peterson*

Acknowledgements

Many thanks to all who helped make this book happen.

Original Guide Editor: Andrew Slade

Photography: Jay Steinke, cover photo and Sam Cook, title page photo.

Project Coordinator: Nancy Hylden (1993 edition), Nancy Odden (1998 and 2001 editions), Gayle Coyer (2004, 2007 and 2010 editions).

Trail Correspondents: Bill Anderson, Jill Dalbacka, Ron Wolff, Bunter Knowles, Don Schlossnagle, Jim Erickson, Ann Russ, Andrew Slade, Ruth Hiland, Karen Hanson, Miriam Graff, Bob Kotz, Bob Fox, Scott Beattie, Rudi Hargesheimer, Heidi Rigelman, John Green, Bill Dryborough, Ken Oelkers, Nancy Odden, Yafa Napadensky, and Joe Panci.

Field Checkers: Mike Anderson, Jim Erickson, Dave Geist, Rudi Hargesheimer, John Kohlstedt, Dick McDermott, Heidi Rigelman, Dick and Ella Slade, Anne and Peter Heegaard, Marilyn Vig, Andrew Slade, Bill Dryborough, Ted Tonkinson, Nancy Odden, Ken Oelkers, Gayle Coyer, and Joe Panci.

Contributing Writers: Deb Shubat, Nancy Hylden, John Green, Lee Radzak, Andrew Slade, Dave Schimpf, Rudi Hargesheimer, Catherine Long, John Kohlstedt, Jeanne Daniels, Anne McKinsey, Cindy Johnson-Groh, Janet Green, and Tricia Ryan.

Book Design and Layout: Sally Rauschenfels

Maps: Matt Kania and Diane Desotelle.

GPS Data: Jeremy Ridlbauer. The project to GPS the trail was funded under the Coastal Zone Management Act, by NOAA's Office of Ocean and Coastal Resource Management, in conjunction with Minnesota's Lake Superior Coastal Program.

Book Production and Proofreading: Catherine Long, Tricia Ryan, Judy Gibbs, Kevin Roalson, Anne McKinsey, Rudi Hargesheimer, Tom Peterson, Kathy Hermes, Nancy Hylden, Jack Morris, Mark Wester, Sally Rauschenfels, Nancy Odden, Ann Possis, Ruth Hiland and Bill Dryborough.

Trail Coodinators: Tom Peterson, Mark Wester, Ken Oelkers, Andrew Slade, Judy Gibbs, Larry Sampson, and Han Taylor.